I0413754

Freedom, Liberty, and Government Overregulation:
A COMPREHENSIVE GUIDE WHY THE POLITICAL LEFT IS NOT GOOD FOR SOCIETY

John Drägonschmidt

First Paperback Edition

Copyright © May 1, 2017
John Drägonschmidt
Freedom, Liberty, and Government Overregulation:
A Comprehensive Guide Why The Political Left Is Not Good For Society

No part of this book may ever be used or reproduced in any type of physical manner whatsoever without written and signed permission from the author and or publisher, except in the case of brief quotations embodied in articles and reviews, along with educational and research purposes. This book may be purchased for educational, research, personal use, business, or sales promotional use.

Copyright © 2017
All rights reserved.

ISBN 10: 1548051985
ISBN-13: 978-1548051983

Non-Fiction—Political Science—Politics—Government,
Liberalism, Government Abuse, Government Overregulation,
Globalism, Trade, Healthcare, Immigration, Law, Climate Change,
Education, Jobs, Taxation, and History

Acknowledgements

This page seeks to acknowledge people, but I am not going to acknowledge the Political Left. Instead, this page will acknowledge those people who like their freedom and liberty. This page will seek to acknowledge who supports the constitution in an originalist and textualist manner. We must acknowledge those who fought for our freedom and liberty as well as those who are still fighting for our freedom and liberty. Since freedom and liberty are under attack by the Political Left, we must make sure that freedom and liberty will never be abolished. We must support and acknowledge the constitution and the declaration of independence, as they represent freedom, liberty, and the pursuit of happiness.

Contents

Freedom, Liberty, and Government Overregulation

John Drägonschmidt

THIS IS NOT A BLANK PAGE BECAUSE IT IS A BLANK PAGE

Introduction

The constitution of the United States of America teaches us that there is and always is a promotion of general welfare of the people, but there are times when the bills passed by Congress and then signed into law by the President are actually against the general welfare of the people. Such laws that go against the promotion of the general welfare of the people not only hurt people but can also be unconstitutional if it forces someone to purchase something that they do not want to purchase.

The constitution and or the general welfare clause does not mandate health insurance or any form of insurance as a human right because the framers and founders of the constitution and the United States of America wanted a very limited government in where people have freedom. Politicians on the left keep stating that health insurance should be a basic human right, but forcing people to buy a product would hurt the general welfare of many people because it forces them to buy a product they might not want but possibly could not afford.

If politicians in the United States of America want a single-payer system for all, then they could simply expand Medicare to every single person, with the exception of illegal and undocumented immigrants and tourists. The reason why those two classes of people should not qualify for the health insurance coverage is because they are not actually legal permanent residents who live and work in the United States of America. Illegal and undocumented immigrants are not here legally, while tourists are only visiting, so those two groups of people should not get the benefits of citizens and legal permanent residents, which is basically the same type of health care system as in Canada.

In addition to if politicians in the United States of America want a single-payer system, then Medicaid should be abolished because it is ineffective and is a poor choice of health insurance. However, with a single-payer system being implemented, the eighty percent payment coverage rate should be kept, as it is fine where it is. At the same time, there will still be health insurance companies in business, as many people might want supplement insurance that will cover the other twenty percent, so this would mean it would be a hybrid single-payer system. Nevertheless, if such a system is to be implemented, then the national debt should be paid off completely.

The problem with Obama Care is that it forces people to buy a product or face a fine, which is clearly unconstitutional, but the Democrats and the Far Left still believe that it is okay and fine to force a person to buy a product they don't want. As a matter of fact, it is not fine, as that is illegal and unconstitutional, yet it is imploding into non-existence because it is a complete failure.

While healthcare might be viewed as an entitlement and a right by the Political Left, the Political Left also supports a globalist trade agenda, as they believe the government should obey special interests that do not support competition. The Political Left's support of a globalist trade agenda is that the small mom-and-pop businesses do not matter. Rather, the Political Left only supports the ideology that big business can succeed, thus the Political Left wants to destroy newer and much smaller companies that provide new business platforms.

Because small mom-and-pop businesses and new small start-up businesses are offering new business platforms, the Political Left sees that as a direct threat to their globalist agenda. The goal of the Political Left globalist trade agenda is to ruin the economic interests of a sovereign nation by replacing it with foreign money and foreign products that over flood the trade market. The Political Left is trying to further their globalist trade agenda because they do not like the interests that support a local and regional economy.

Instead, the Political Left wants everything to be replaced with foreign interests. The Political Left seeks to undermine the local and regional economies because they do not like those types of economies. Yet, the Political Left seeks to believe that only the United Nations matter. But, the Political Left needs to remember that they need to understand that the local and regional economies are what drive the backbone of their countries. A globalist economy will only benefit the foreign nations who are over flooding the domestic markets, thus the United States of America economy will be ruined by foreign interests.

This brings us to culture and free speech, as the Political Left will make an attempt to destroy the past and to replace it with their own radical and extremist values and beliefs that supports communism, fascism, socialism, anarchy, and Marxism. The Political Left simply does not like white people, as the Political Left constantly believes that white people are the problems of all people, even though many of the Political Left is actually white.

The Political Left does not really like white people, so they created a faction of what is known as social justice warriors, and these social justice warriors attempt to claim that white people are terrorizing them around the world. These claims from the social justice warriors are just insane and ridiculous, as the social justice warriors do not like the history of the world so they seek to change it by rioting in the streets and breaking the law.

The Political Left and this Political Left faction of social justice warriors seeks to undermine the freedom of expression of anyone who is white. The Political Left seeks to infringe on cultural values on white people as well as trying to take away the freedom of celebration from anyone who is white or of European descent. The Political Left seeks to think that a white person should not be able to celebrate the holidays of different countries but the Political Left also thinks it is racist and offensive to eat and make different cultural and ethnic dishes in a different manner.

The Political Left makes up too many excuses to be offended about, as they probably don't live in reality, aka the real world. The Political Left seeks to replace culture with their own safe-space versions, yet they will also seek to undermine free speech, as the Political Left only believes they have the right to free speech. If you do not agree with the Political Left your free speech is automatically named as hate speech, as the reason is due to the Political Left does not want to hear differing opinions. This is what is known as liberal lunacy, which is simply the undermining of freedom of expression and freedom of liberty.

The Political Left constantly engages in liberal lunacy, as they seek to infringe on your constitutional rights guaranteed by God and the bill of rights as well as the rest of the constitution. The Political Left will resort to name calling if they don't agree with you and they will make an attempt to shut your free speech down. The Political Left just hates reality, and they even demand their education should be in the form of an entitlement funded by the government. The reason why the Political Left wants free education is because they want access to free money and they believe they do not have to repay anything.

The Political Left is harming college students, as the Political Left professors want to indoctrinate the students with views that support socialism, Marxism, communism, fascism, and anarchy; yet many students are already part of the Political Left. The Political Left does not live in reality, as when they get a job, they might find it difficult to work with people of different ideologies, and this is what happens when children are constantly coddled in a safe-space with no mention of reality.

Education is supposed to be a place of intellectual discussions and of new ideas, but the Political Left demands everything a safe space. The Political Left college students will find that it is difficult to work in the real world once they find a job, as people have different beliefs, opinions, values, and views. And, you can't just call a person racist and or xenophobic just because they have a different ideology, as that person could have first-hand experience of the problem; yet the Political Left will probably ignore this and start calling you names for no reasons just because you have a different opinion. Nevertheless, it is simply amazing that the Political Left does not understand reality, as they believe taxes are too low.

The Political Left claims that the rich are not paying their fair share, and so they believe that the rich should pay more taxes, even more than the highest tax bracket. The Political Left says this about taxes because they want the rich to pay all of the taxes so that the Political Left can use that money for a free handout such as welfare and to fund social welfare programs. Yet, the Political Left only wants this free money because they don't want to work but instead wants to cheat the government.

And if that is not enough, the Political Left thinks that they can get away with cheating the system, even though other hard deserving people actually earned that money. The Political Left just does not want to work for their money, as they seek to just collect a paycheck from the federal government. And so, if they get free money from the government, well why would they even want to work, well the answer is they don't want to work.

The reason why the Political Left does not want to work is due to the fact that they support big government and they believe government is the solution to everything. Nevertheless, when it is about immigration and climate change, the Political Left decides that they are not going to be lazy.

The Political Left is not lazy when they support open borders and that illegal immigrants should never be deported. The Political Left is just hypocritical. They believe that illegal immigrants should be entitled to citizenships, even though the illegal immigrants have violated the law when they arrived here: by crossing the border illegally. Then, when illegal immigrants actually commit crimes within their new country, they still gain support from the Political Left, as the Political Left believes it is fine to harbor illegal immigrants from immigration officials.

The Political Left tries to do all they can to obstruct the entire system, yet they do not support illegal immigrants being deported, but this is not a surprise. But, if you think about it, the Political Left does not want to uphold immigration law, yet the Political Left does not want to conduct new research in regards to climate change, as the Political Left believes that the climate question is settled.

However, the climate question is not settled, as the Political Left always wants to manipulate the research to their political beliefs and views. To make matters worse, the Political Left wants to blame humans as the problem of everything, yet humans are actually not the problem, and neither is carbon dioxide. But even worse, if you ever decide to develop a differing view on climate change than the Political Left, well you might be prosecuted or even persecuted for your own beliefs.

Yes, you heard that correctly, the Political Left will make an attempt to prosecute you for your beliefs. The Political Left will also make an attempt to take away your freedom and liberty because they want to abuse their power. The Political Left is just politically corrupt, as they have no respect for freedom and liberty. But when it comes to the Political Left, well they only support their freedom and liberty, yet the Political Left does not care about other peoples' freedom and or liberty, as the Political Left is hypocritical and wants to undermine the entire constitution.

As you read this book, I hope that you remember the founding and the traditional principles of the federalist papers, the constitution, and the declaration of independence of the United States of America. You must remember that freedom, liberty, and rights come from God, as no other country does this.

In the United States of America we have the most freedom, liberty, and rights, and you should respect that because of what America stands for. No other country has the same amount of freedom, liberty, and rights as the United States of America; and this should allow you to think that freedom and liberty are constantly being attacked by fascists, socialists, communists, Marxists, and anarchists, and all of these support violence, but none of them support freedom and liberty because they all engage in criminal acts.

So, just remember, don't take freedom and liberty for granted, as you could be actually living in a country that supports Antifa fascism, as Antifa does engage in fascism and violent criminal acts. You should respect the freedom and liberty that you have in the United States of America. Remember, freedom and liberty isn't free, as the United States fought for their freedom from a brutal Great Britain at the time of the eighteenth century.

Nevertheless, defending freedom and liberty comes at a cost, as there will always be threats that seek to undermine our freedom and liberty of the United States of America. We need to make sure that no enemy escapes justice. We need to support the soldiers and the veterans who fought for and are continuing to fight for our freedom and liberty. We must always support the constitution and the declaration of independence of the United States of America.

Libertatem libertas parta est

Thank you for your purchase,
John Drägonschmidt

Chapter One

Globalism, Trade, and Healthcare

I mproving coverage to people who did not have

coverage or to people who were not able to get coverage because of their pre-existing condition was a major goal for the Affordable Care Act. While providing a ban on lifetime limits is good, that is not the worse of the actual law. The worse part of the law was the individual and employer mandates, as it forced people (including businesses and individuals) to purchase insurance for them and or their employers (for a business with at least 50 fulltime employees) or to face a fine.

The road to a proper health care policy is important, as many people believe that it should be a universal right. However, in the United States of America, health care is not a universal right, since the founders and the framers of the United States of America and its constitution did not want the government to be in everyone's lives, as they believe any type of government that is too big will erode the values of freedom. The goal of the founders and the framers were to set up and to establish a very limited government that granted certain and specific freedoms from God, since it was God who was the creator of all life and allowed people to live in order to survive. Yet, the rights that were granted by God predated the constitution of the United States of America and were from the declaration of independence. But, the idea of these God-given rights was because of virtue, as the ideology of rights originating from government could be taken away. So, rights were deemed as being originated from God because a fear of government abusing its power in regards to freedom.

The goal of the United States of America declaration of independence and the constitution was to limit any possible government overreach and abuse and to set a national framework of what people would expect of government. Indeed, the declaration of independence and the constitution have been trampled upon over the years by people from many factions, as they believe it should be considered a living document. However, this living document garbage is ignorant, as the founders and the framers of the country wanted and expected the government and the leaders of the government to actually follow the true and original meaning of the documents, as freedom and liberty were the true meanings.

So, how does this all play into healthcare policy, well liberals, democrats, and anyone who demands healthcare be considered constitutional rights are mistaken about the constitution and the declaration of independence, as there is no mention of it in any document? God does not expect everyone to have everything and he would not support something that oppresses people, such as the mandate that forces people to purchase something they don't need. That is in fact that is actually unconstitutional because the mandate forces a person to purchase something they don't want or they will face a fine, which can be described as oppression.

In fact, countries who believe healthcare should be God-given rights actually determine what rights you do and do not have, as those countries believe rights, freedom, and liberty are determined by the government. Now, many people in the United States of America are entitled to free healthcare, but that would be due to them being a veteran, but not all veterans receive free healthcare.[1] On the other hand, seniors who are at least 65 years of age receive a form of medical insurance that pays for hospital and doctor visits, called Medicare, but that only covers 80% of the cost. If a senior wanted complete coverage they would need to purchase a supplement plan

---

[1] U.S. Department of Veterans Affairs, Health Benefits, https://www.va.gov/healthbenefits/cost/.

for the other 20% not including a separate plan for prescriptions, as drugs are not even covered when purchased at an in-store pharmacy.

You could say that Medicare could be expanded to become a single-payer system, but there is a problem with that. The problem is that government can be ineffective at deciding who can get an appointment, surgery, or something else. The services could be rationed as there are cutoff times. But the main issue is because of the national debt and spending. If the government reduced its national debt to nothing being owed, then it would be fine, but the government must also make a surplus before it can use and institute such a program, as anything can cause a deficit. However, the federal government is not really known for keeping and maintaining a surplus, as all they care about is spending because they want an unlimited supply of money. The expanded program of Medicare for all will cause the government to grow bankrupt if costs are not controlled.

Consequently, with limited amounts of money, healthcare would be rationed, but many poor people have something known as Medicaid, but Medicaid is very insufficient because of its coverage rate. So, to expand Medicare for all, one must first consider the costs of not just Medicare but also of Medicaid, as a single-payer system would have to eliminate one of these programs. Medicare is more efficient than Medicaid, but both programs do not completely cover every amount of costs, as there are still some out-of-pocket expenses. Still, if the national debt gets paid off, then there can be some sort of Medicare expansion that will cover every single qualified person, but to support such an expansion there needs to be some sort of tax to support and to maintain it, or else it will just become a blank check from the government that wastes money.

Now, what would happen to that healthcare from the U.S Department of Veteran Affairs, well nothing? If there is a single-payer system, then Medicare for all will replace anyone who has Medicaid. At the same time, Medicare would replace any health insurance held by anyone. However, even though everyone will be covered by Medicare who are eligible, people might still buy health insurance, as they might want an alternative to government-funded insurance and or they might just want a supplement plan to cover any costs that might not be included in the program.

The key issue is funding, and as of this writing, it would be extremely inappropriate and reckless to institute such a program, as the national debt is out of control and our politicians want to keep on spending money without any regard for paying down any amount of the national debt. If such a program is instituted, and there is a lack of money because of an extremely high national debt and constant spending, then people will start to protest in the streets about it and they will demand recall elections because those politicians are wasting the money of the government. The liberals and anyone else who supports such a program will be praising the politicians, as they believe socialism in all forms is good for the country. But, socialism means freedom is taken away from each individual, as now the government will be able to control the healthcare system. So, in order to eliminate such a problem, the health insurance industry must still exist, as people need to have a choice between a tax-payer government plan and the alternative choice of paying for insurance without any government subsidy. But, the people who support socialism might have a problem with the alternate choice because they do not like capitalism and businesses making a profit and revenue.

Yet, the recent presidential election victory in France by Emmanuel Macron would seem that socialists do support capitalism. But, in the model of the French election that gave Macron his very wide margin of victory, it seems this version of capitalism is not actually the real meaning of capitalism. Instead, this pseudo-capitalism is known as globalism, also known as globalization, and by this meaning, there is only support to expand another foreign government entity on the actual government. So, this means that the actual state government (France) will not be revitalized, since the goal is to expand the powers of the European Union on France. This basically means that the European Unions will make the decisions for France and that France will lose its culture and sovereignty because jobs will now be outsourced to a different country, probably in Europe.

Globalism instead supports the idea that external outside forces should be in control and that the internal or domestic forces or laws do not matter. Therefore, globalists believe that small businesses are not that well equipped to survive, because small businesses are only there to exist the local population and any people who visit their company or business storefront to purchase

15

something or to look around and browse. Now, there is nothing wrong with globalism if you want to participate in the international markets and to expand your business, but when the government supports globalism it is a bad idea. When the government supports globalism it is a bad, dangerous, and reckless idea because the government is now supporting an idea that goes against any and all domestic policies. Instead, the government supports policy driven by a foreign entity that is not the centralized government of that country. To put it into context, the European Union supports a globalist ideology and wants to dictate the rules and laws of France, and they believe their laws are superior over France because France is just a country with a government that provides support for businesses and future opportunities for employment. The reason for their logic of supporting globalism is because it provides thousands and millions of jobs, and that big business is better because more jobs are provided and it supports competition.

However, the globalists keep on failing to understand that small businesses are the backbone of the communities and provide the majority of the competition. Small businesses cannot really compete with the practices of the big businesses. Essentially, the argument to support globalism is that small businesses will never improve the economy of the world because small businesses only help their local and state economies. Instead, globalists believe the world economy is better than world economies, as there is a need to interact with each part of the world. Well, that argument is clearly irrational, as small businesses do help the world economy, but small businesses believe that the world economies should not be above that of the local and state growth. What the globalists support is an ideology that the world economy is superior to the local and state economies, as the globalists believe that the world economies are very essential to helping the small people. Yet, the globalists fear that small businesses will become more prominent and that government should support international and foreign interests over domestic interests. You see, the globalists hate the promotion of any type of domestic interest and policies, as the globalists want outside and international interests to dictate any domestic interests to the sovereign country. The bottom line is that globalists support the idea that the citizens and the legal residents of the populace and the sovereign country should come last, as the globalists believe international and outside interests should always be first. This simply means that the governments and people who support globalism will not stand up for their own people, as they want to defend global interests because they believe domestic issues are irrelevant to helping the country and the people to succeed. The logic of the globalists is that international and outside interest will always help the interests of the country and their populace, but this is irrational behavior, as only domestic interests and policies can help the country and the populace to succeed, since it is the country and or its government for providing job and employment opportunities within the country.

Although, this makes the socialists look like hypocrites, because you thought they opposed everything that is capitalism and globalism. Well, one described socialist-like politician by the name of

Bernie Sanders does not like the idea of globalism, and his policies are usually in line with socialist ideas. Bernie Sanders is simply a politician who believes globalism hurts the national economy of a country, and he is probably right, as the goal of globalism, as already mentioned, is to usurp the national interests of a sovereign country and to replace it with international and outside global interests that benefit the rest of the world. So in essence, every other country will benefit from those interests except for that one lonely country whose government leaders believed globalism would benefit their own national interests. But instead, that lonely country would receive little or no benefits at all because those benefits will go to the rest of the world. This simply means that those promised benefits to that one particular country were actually stolen by the rest of the world because of some lobbyist who believes everything should be free to the world. In fact, these lobbyists might be paid by large corporations who support globalism, but their ideology is to only support globalism by influencing the government to accept the process and role of globalism. In other words, the lobbyist will tell the governments that globalism must be supported by the government and the country because it will actually benefit the country as a whole, but they forget to mention that globalism will actually take away many jobs from that country, which would then hurt the economy and will then cause a recession. The populace will then turn against the government for supporting and creating a plan that institutes globalism, because everything failed.

Now, what has caused this shift in globalism, well, as explained before, it is simply because small business is too inferior to grow. Yet, this excuse is proven false, as Amazon, Apple, KFC, and other companies were once small businesses, and they grew into large corporations because of meeting a growth for demand. This simply means that if a particular person starts a specific type of company, then people might buy products from that company, and potentially that company will grow and become very successful. But the globalists' assertion of supporting globalism is that it is necessary for progress and change, something that the Democrats and Far Left explain is good for everyone. But, the progress and changes demanded by people who like and lean towards a globalist ideology do not want competition because they see it as a threat to their own company. On the other hand, the Democrats and the Far Left who support and demand progress and change see it as a matter of a mandate of changing the traditional values to more radical values. In other words, Progressives and Liberals would like to replace the traditional founding American principles of the constitution and the declaration of independence with something such as free entitlements for all. This will cause more debt and it does nothing for trade, but actually supports the idea of globalism is good for the country. The thing about globalism is that it hurts fair trade as the large companies take advantage of abusing free trade because of governments agreeing to bad trade deals.

There is nothing wrong with free trade, but if countries continue to abuse the trade process, then something must be done to prevent that from occurring again. In order to support and initiate better trade policies, one must consider the dangerous consequences of globalism and globalist thinking, as anything that supports globalism can have bad consequences for the countries who initiate a globalist trade deal. The idea is that multi-lateral trade deals are better than bilateral trade deals, but the former actually is bad because it includes and asserts that a one-size-fits-all approach to every country will be beneficial. In fact, not every country is the same, as each requires different things, so it would be better to institute one-on-one or bilateral trade deals, as these are more focused. However, globalists see it differently, as they want as few trade deals as possible, as they believe if an entire region of countries can be included in the trade agreement, then it would lead prosperity to all. But, the globalists fail to understand that instead of America getting those jobs that were promised, they will instead go to one of those many other countries that were part of the deal. Remember, the globalists tend to believe a one-size-fits-all model is appropriate, but not every country has the same needs as other countries. Vietnam and South Korea are not the same, and they tend to have different necessities, just like the United States of America.

But, the globalists do not care about this, as they want to flood the trade market with extremely cheap goods, products, and services. This mass-market amount of extremely cheap goods, products, and services will hurt the local economies of each city, state, and county, and will only benefit the country that produces them such as China, India, or Pakistan. Essentially, the globalists believe this theory of mass over production will actually benefit each country, but in fact it has the opposite effect. It will only help the countries that produce those high amounts of market overproduction of goods, products, and services, as there is now a flooding of the market. This means that trade between each of the countries will become too uncompetitive, as one of the countries flood the market with too many products, goods, and services, and this will undercut those specific goods, products, and services in the country that receives them, such as China exporting steel to the United States of America. Since, so much of a particular product, good, or service is exported by one country, it does undercut the value of those similar goods, products, and services in the receiving country, as the exporting country could be doing this because the company that produces these materials in that foreign country might actually be heavily funded or subsidized by local and or the central/national governments. Now, if you explain this to the globalists, they might agree with this, but most likely they will say this is a false assertion even though they know it is true. The fact of the matter is that the people who support globalism do not want to admit the truth about what it does to the economies of other countries. The globalists fail to see the negative consequences of globalism, as they do not support any type of local economies, including small businesses. The globalists will try to do all they can to discredit fair trade, as they want everything to be free so that they can flood the trade markets with cheap and poorly made goods, services, and products, and some that could actually be knockoffs or pirated.

Freedom, Liberty, and Government Overregulation

One must thing that the globalists might be clueless about their trade policies, but they are probably not, yet many of them are clueless because they fail to acknowledge the reality that globalism has on any local or state economy. Flooding the trade markets is beneficial to them because the globalists believe it enhances competition, which might be true, but it floods the trade markets with too many items to choose from because a government subsidizing all items in a specific category will essentially cause a market reaction that undercuts all other similar items from other countries. This basically means that country A might make too much money because they flooded the trade markets of country B, and this essentially means country B might fail to meet its quotas for each quarter.

This lack of quotas would further lead to a lack of economic growth, as there will be too many foreign items in a domestic market, and businesses domiciled in the United States of America would lose too much money if this practice of globalist trade does not end. The thing about globalist trade, as mentioned before, is that it takes away the real competition and replaces it with cheap knockoffs that are very inferior to the real goods, services, and or products. These globalist trade items are practically imitations, and if you can physically touch them, it is highly likely that they will break apart very easily, because they are actually fake or even stolen. Too many products, goods, or services from foreign countries will only hurt the economy of the receiving country because it is too much inventory for the receiving country to handle. The amount of inventory exported by the foreign country to the receiving country would potentially overwhelm the trade markets that essentially the most seen item would replace the better one. This simply means that even though the items are the same, everyone will always but the foreign one because there is a lack of domestic inventory due to the foreign inventory items completely flooding the entire trade markets. Now, the globalists won't agree with this, since any store will always make money, but this is not about stores making money, even if the bigger stores always put the smaller stores out of business. Instead, this is about governments and countries flooding the trade markets with their cheap inventory because of globalism, and by simply doing this constantly, the receiving country will never likely have a fair chance to compete.

The globalist trade agenda just outsources everything to a cheaper country, and the government of that country will try to export too much inventory to gain an unfair amount of competition, which is also an unfair advantage. This unfair advantage makes it unfair for the receiving country to compete because the exporting country is knowingly sabotaging any chances of the receiving country to make any money. The one thing for sure is that the globalists want to undercut the trade markets of the receiving countries in order to benefit themselves, as they have nothing better to do. They simply have no shame because they just want to promote their globalist agendas in order to promote them. This simply means the globalists only care about their globalist priorities because they want to make a name for themselves just to undercut everyone else. The globalists know exactly what they are doing to hurt the receiving countries, but they do not care that they are always constantly over flooding the trade markets in order to undercut the local and state performance. You see, the globalists only care about their case of supporting international trade and not local businesses. They simply cannot understand why the local businesses are better than their globalist agenda.

This globalist agenda might be bad, but it can be dangerous for anyone who simply cannot compete. That is because the globalists do not like competition at all, since they believe competition will ruin their business model of having foreign governments flood countries with cheap inventory. The globalists make money as part of their consulting fee, while the governments are able to profit by essentially buying up all of the available spaces in the trade markets because they only want people to buy their products. The precise logic of the globalists is crazy and ill-informed, because they believe only they should be in business, as they tend to say it is a changing world and that only the big and powerful can and will should survive. This logic is potentially and most likely ignorant, as it is safe to say they might listen to outside opinion, but when listening they will probably ignore it and say it does not make sense when you finally ask them about their overall reasoning. It is precisely the reason why it is hard to convince them, as they do not want to accept change. Instead, the globalists believe change is a terrible idea that will decrease prices. This isn't surprising, as the globalists exist in all markets, such as in the oil industry, also known as OPEC. In the case of OPEC, recently, as of this writing, they demanded the United States of America to decrease oil production because it is hurting their production of oil, since they want to actually and believe they can control the prices of a barrel of oil.[2] Now, OPEC claims that they simply want to balance the oil market,[3] but that is just an excuse by saying that they are unhappy that the oil prices are too low. Instead, the true intention of OPEC is to decrease oil production in order to raise prices, as many countries cannot survive because they heavily relied upon and instituted a globalist agenda. You see, the problem with OPEC's globalist agenda is that they want to dictate the price of oil by limiting its supply, as they believe it is a threat and too dangerous to have too much oil on the market, and they want every single country to follow this system. Instead, the United States of America ignores this proposed system and ideology, as they are their own sovereign country, and as a sovereign country, the United States of America does not want to give up its own independence. On the other hand, under President Obama and the Democrats, they essentially gave up America's status as a sovereign nation, as the Obama Administration and the Democrats believed the United Nations is superior to the law of the United States of America. The Democrats believe the United Nations should replace the constitution of the United States of America and the declaration of

---

[2] Ivana Kottasová, "OPEC to U.S.: Please don't pump so much oil!," *CNN Money*, May 11, 2017, http://money.cnn.com/2017/05/11/investing/opec-oil-u-s-supply/.

[3] Ibid

independence, as they see it is a threat to their globalist agenda, even though some of them might claim they are actually against globalism.

This support of globalism is not new, as the globalist agenda aims to undermine traditional American values with that of values from the rest of the world. In other words, the values prescribed by the constitution and the declaration of independence would be replaced with values that support communism, socialism, and Marxism, which are all part of the same branch of political theory. Instead, globalists don't believe in the values of the two documents, as they see it is a threat to globalism, since they want to bypass the legal process and take it to a place with no jurisdiction over the matter. This simply means that the globalists and or the Democrats believe the United Nations should charge you with a crime. But yet another problem with the United Nations is that they want to undermine the Bill of Rights, and in particular, the Second Amendment, as they believe guns and or any type of firearms should be regulated by an international body. Not only is that unconstitutional, but it also violates the sovereign status of the United States of America. Yet, the United Nations and their globalist agenda do not really care about that, as under the leadership of the Obama Administration, the United Nations has usurped the power of the United States of America at least two times, since Obama requested to avoid the proper way. The proper way that was ignored was the fact that the Obama administration did not get two treaties ratified by the Senate, as he knew they would not get approval. These two treaties that did not get Senate ratification were the Iranian

Agreement and the Paris Climate Change Agreement. Both treaties must be ratified by the Senate, and both are actually treaties, since they are actually agreements between foreign countries and the United States of America.

The two treaties mentioned above never actually begun in the Senate, as the Obama bypassed everything to the United Nations, and their goal was intentionally to never send it to the Senate, because they complained of having trouble with getting the required votes to pass it in the Senate. The Obama administration was just using that as an excuse, as a treaty will be passed by the Senate, if looks good and is good for both countries, not just for the foreign country. Now, Congress has passed many treaties, including the North American Free Trade Agreement (NAFTA), but Congress does not usually read them, and so no one will ever know what is in those treaties unless they read them. So, this would seem that the Congress does not care because they believe it actually benefits America. In fact, as probably mentioned before, a bilateral or one-on-one treaty with another country and America is the best choice, since anything involving more than two countries would lead to problems. Only now, as of this writing, are politicians in the United States of America are figuring out that multilateral agreements are bad, but this is not shared universally, as many Democrats support a globalist agenda, because they want to benefit their pockets.

Now, this is no secret about the Democrats and their globalist agenda, as Obama was one of the most famous globalists, but they are hypocrites because they are actually anti-business, since they demand higher taxes on everyone, which they will deny. Sure, they always deny everything, and they will make up an excuse or distort the truth, like they always constantly do. They also take everything out of context, because they don't like what other people say about their ideologies, but their opponents are just stating the facts. In other circumstances, if a Democrat claims they are taken out of context, they are probably wrong, because this was confirmed with Hillary Clinton and her globalist agenda that she refuses to accept. For instance, Clinton who ran for President and lost badly to Donald Trump clearly stated she wanted the coal miners fired by getting rid of the entire coal mining industry, but then she said that was taken out of context and the Anti-Trump media agreed with her. The thing behind this though is that Clinton, the Democrats, and the Radical Far Left do not support coal mining, as they believe it hurts the environment, even though not must exists. Further, the reason why Democrats, Clinton, and other Far Left people want to get rid of the coal mining industry is because they are globalists of the alternative energy platform, as they believe windmills and solar panels are safer. Now, there is nothing wrong with alternative energy practices, but these people on the Left-hand side of the political spectrum want to eliminate coal altogether, and they make a claim for health and safety, but really they are just shills who are against the natural resources of the planet. It is important to use these resources because they might provide better amounts of efficiency, since no wind or sun is required of them. The health concern is amusing at best, since coal miners actually know what they are getting into at their jobs. The coal miners are really good at their jobs, and they want to work in that particular industry because it provides them with support and comfort, but also because the people working in that industry actually want to work in that particular industry. Yet, the people who align themselves as being on the Left-side of the political spectrum do not care about this, and they fail to understand this issue, since they are simply out of touch with reality. They believe that coal is a bad idea, but many coal miners are actually Democrats, and when they heard politicians attacking coal mining, the coal miners decided to vote for Donald Trump, but the Democrats think coal is a bad source of energy. Let us remind everyone that the Sun is not always shining and that sometimes there is a lack of wind, but the Democrats do not care about this, because they think health is more superior to people making a living. However, without making money, there would probably be no access to insurance available to many people, since many people were not raised as trust-fund babies or born with a silver spoon in their mouths. Yet, health is important, but the Democrats do not get the role of a limited government, as they demand the government control everything, unless they do not like a particular idea. But, they do have one thing in common with each other, and that is promoting a government-run health care insurance system. Nevertheless, if you are Senator Dianne Feinstein, you will get booed at by your own political party, because again, the people on the Far Left always demand they should be entitled to everything, as they believe everything should be a right.

From one perspective, single-payer might be good, but it is very costly, and can get out of control. The proposed single-payer system that I outlined in here is actually not single-payer because eligible people will still have to pay or foot twenty percent of the coverage, since Medicare would only pay eighty percent of the care provided. Now, there is more to this, as health care does need attention, but one part to mention is that once a person gets the bill from treatment or after from being discharged, the amount of money owed should be decreased. At present time, after an eligible person is discharged, they will owe a payment of no more and no less than $1,316.00,[4] and a payment negotiation might be appropriate between the eligible person and the hospital, but I believe this payment should be lowered to no higher than $550.00 and no lower than $235.00. By implementing somewhere in between these two lower payments, it is better for the people who are on Medicare, and it would be suitable even more if Medicare for all was established. But, to institute such a program for all U.S. Citizens and legal permanent residents would require a major overhaul, and this includes paying off all of the outstanding national debt. Once all of the national debt is paid off, you must institute some sort of way that it will be paid for in order to finance the program. Such funding for a program would require a new tax being implemented, and it should be noted that you will probably never notice this tax because it will be included as part of your income taxes. Now, this is possibly the only way to maintain the

---

[4] United States Government, Medicare 2017 costs at a glance, https://www.medicare.gov/your-medicare-costs/costs-at-a-glance/costs-at-glance.html.

Medicare for all system, as if no changes occur to the current Medicare system, it will go bankrupt. So, the Medicare system will go bankrupt, unless Congress can decrease the national debt to a reasonable amount, which I recommend is zero dollars.

In order to do anything, there must always be change, as the current health care and insurance system is outdated. Instead of going to a Medicare for all system, one must currently think about the alternative options, such as opening up insurance to state lines. Now, everyone should be able to purchase health insurance, but no one should be denied because they have a pre-existing condition. The coverage should be reasonable and there should be no lifetime limits. At the same time, no one should be forced to purchase something they don't want. But, the most important thing here is opening up insurance across state lines, but Democrats and their alleged pseudo-analysists actually oppose that because they say it won't decrease costs.[5] Now, the main reasoning the Democrats and the people on the Far Left assert is that they think that the conservatives and Republicans are expecting health insurance premiums to drop by at least one-hundred percent. However, the conservatives and Republicans do know that the premiums will never be that low, as they want them to be reasonable, so it is possible that some premiums could go down as much as sixty percent, but the hope is that it will go down to twenty or even forty percent. Remember folks,

---

[5] Alex Tolbert, "Why Selling Insurance Across State Lines Won't Work," *Huffington Post*, April 19, 2016, http://www.huffingtonpost.com/alex-tolbert/why-selling-insurance-across_b_9719986.html.

just because insurance is open to anyone across state lines that do not mean it will automatically decrease to outlandish and extremely low prices. No, what opening up health insurance across state lines means is that the premiums will be available to purchase at reasonable prices. Yet, the people on the Left side of the political spectrum demand prices be affordable, but their reasoning behind affordable is that it must include every single thing that should be covered even if not needed, but this actually drives prices and costs up, since there are too many items (conditions) to be covered that are unnecessary for the purchaser. So, you think the Left will get it, but their affordable scheme to health care and health insurance does not do anything but increases everything and makes it difficult for insurers to earn enough money. Now, the people on the Left believe there is nothing wrong with this, as they still believe it is necessary, but they are arrogant and ignorant, because they know the Affordable Care act is imploding, and it is probably going to be replaced after this book is released, hopefully by something written by Texas Senator Ted Cruz, who has been working on a better piece of legislation than that of the House of Representatives. On the other hand, the Democrats and the Far Left believe that the Affordable Care Act is an excellent law, but the problem with that is it imposes a mandate to purchase insurance, and if you don't have insurance you will be subject to a penalty. Well, not everyone can afford to purchase insurance, and forcing a penalty or fine on someone for not purchasing a product is the same as a court-mandated fine. The Democrats and the Far Left want to automatically convict you of not having health insurance, and so they included a penalty that is considered to be just plainly unconstitutional. On the other hand, the court-mandated fine is legal and constitutional because you are actually in a court of law for some sort of legal problems, such as breaking the law. But, the Democrats and the Far Left want to make not having health insurance a crime because they believe everyone should be forced to purchase a product, even if they don't like it.

Still, the Democrats and the Far Left want to simply reform the Affordable Care Act, but not for the reasons you think. You see, they know it is a bad law but they only want to make it extremely worse, and not even thinking about any consequences such as the national debt. On the other hand, the conservatives and the Republicans understand that the Affordable Care Act is an extremely bad law, and they know that it will and is currently out of control and is possibly already imploding, so they are trying to get rid of it as best as they can. Now, the conservatives and the Republicans understand that the premiums are skyrocketing, but if you tell that to the Democrats and the Far Left they will simply say any increase is only an isolated cost. Now, you can see the differences here, as they know it is not an isolated cost, as they know deductibles are so outrageous, but simply stated, the Democrats and the Far Left do not care. The only place you might be able to use such a high deductible is a hospital, as regular doctor visits are extremely cheap when compared to a hospital stay, since hospitals always jack up the prices on everything, but I say you could still pay that high deductible to the hospital because they want their money fast. Of course, the

Democrats and the Far Left will attempt to dispute the rising deductibles, as they will keep saying it is only an isolated case, when in reality it is increasing everywhere, so they will always attempt to discredit people. This has always been a tactic by the Democrats and the Far Left because they do not want to accept the responsibility of anything that went wrong. In fact, as of this writing, the Democrats and the Far Left already created another victim due to the Affordable Care Act, as it is reported that Aetna is now going to exit all marketplaces by 2018, and so, the Democrats and the Far Left would like to bury this. Instead, an architect of the Affordable Care Act blames President Trump and the Republicans, as their excuse is that Trump and the Republicans never gave the law a chance and used fear to say it is not working. In fact, the Affordable Care Act is not working, as it has never worked. The reason why it hasn't work is because the Democrats and Far Left did a horrible job of writing it, and then they decided that Obama's promise of keeping your current doctor and health insurance plan did not matter. How did they do this, well, they included too much stuff that didn't need to be included in the coverage. The Democrats and the Far Left made it illegal to purchase cheap health insurance because they believe in a one-size-fits-all model, as they believe in America health insurance is a right. Well, here is one thing for sure, and that is they kept on asserting Mitt Romney did the same exact thing in the same as Massachusetts. The problem with comparing the health insurance system mandate in Massachusetts with that of the Federal Government is that the former is just a state while the latter includes the entire country, meaning there is less people in a state than a country, but the Democrats and the Far Left refuse to admit this, as they are constantly obsessed with universal health care and a single-payer system. Their logic seems amazing, but personally, I also believe that this mandate in Massachusetts is also unconstitutional because it forces you to purchase a product that you might not need. Now, as there might be some logic behind this, there is surely some basis for health care and the entire health insurance system to be reformed, but the reason on how to reform them is questionable from the Democrats and the members of the Far Left.

Now, let's look at some countries with universal health care, as you want to know more about them so you will understand them better. We will begin with Canada. In Canada, only legal permanent residents and citizens can get access to free health care, but you must sign up for it in your local province, but not everything is free.[6] In Canada, if you go to a different province to seek health care, you might be charged a fee; but basically, health care is based upon each province, and since each of them are different, you might have to wait longer to gain access to the system.[7] Yet, free emergency services are always offered, but you must have a health care insurance card by the government to gain full access to all eligible services offered; however, there is also the option of purchasing private insurance if you do not have public health insurance or if you need

---

[6] Government of Canada, Health care in Canada, http://www.cic.gc.ca/english/newcomers/after-health.asp.

[7] Ibid

health insurance to cover some procedure or other item that is not covered by public health insurance, such as prescription drugs, dental care, or vision care, but these are basically considered to be extended health care insurance plans.[8] So, if you think about it, Canada does not actually offer universal health care, because you need to buy private health insurance just to purchase your prescription drugs if you are ever prescribed such medication by your medical doctor.[9] Now, isn't it funny how Democrats and members of the Far Left always proclaim how great a country Canada is for having universal health care, even though it does not provide free ambulance services and medication as part of the coverage.[10]

Yet, now we shall explore the United Kingdom, with a focus on just the National Health Services of England, which is as of now of this writing, has problems with a Ransomware problem due to hackers demanding money. So, let's explore the British health care system and how it covers and cares for people. In England, the NHS can be a bit complicated to understand, as the free services are usually offered to just residents and UK citizens who live or reside within England.[11] Now, if you are just a visitor from another country, you will have some access for free as part of Britain's NHS universal

---

[8] Ibid

[9] Ibid

[10] Ibid

[11] About Travel, Can Visitors Use Free UK Medical Services?, http://gouk.about.com/od/tripplanning/p/emergencydoctor.htm.

health care coverage, but this is just limited to emergency treatment,[12] such as if you just need a cast for your arm or leg. In other words, the only free treatment a person receives in the NHS hospital is emergency treatment, such as in an emergency room, and this is probably to prevent medical tourism, as some people might only seek treatment there because of free health care being available.[13] On the other hand, if you are a visitor, once you have been admitted to the actual hospital, you will have to pay a fee, and this is the case even though you might need surgery, as well as any drugs, and this is again probably to eliminate medical tourism.[14] Now, any visitor does have free access to have certain infectious diseases treated, HIV testing, mandated psychiatric treatment, and a few other services.[15] For visitors who live in the other parts of the European Economic Area and visit England, they might have more free access to the NHS system, as certain agreements have to be in place to have free access, but this might expand to some NATO employees.[16] Nevertheless, visitors who need prescription drugs once admitted to the hospital need to pay the full amount of about £1,000 [17] instead of the

---

[12] Ibid

[13] Ibid

[14] Ibid

[15] Ibid

[16] Ibid

[17] Ibid

subsidized amount of £8.60 per item.[18] For anyone who lives in England, it is a very low amount of money to pay for prescription medication, but it is free for anyone who meets certain criteria, such as being under the age of sixteen, being age sixty or over, have income support, a patient at an inpatient NHS hospital, and many more classifications of people, including "medicines personally administered by a GP or provided via a Patient Group Direction (PGD), as well as "Medicines administered at a hospital or an NHS walk-in centre."[19] Now, if you are a resident of England and live there, you might be entitled to travel reimbursements, if you meet one of three options, which will not be explained here; but if you qualify for a low income scheme you might gain access to reduced prescription drugs, reduced vision and dental costs, reduced travel costs, and or something associated with reduced costs of wigs and fabrics.[20] So, what have we learned about the universal health care and insurance system in England, well, it is more universal than that in Canada, and it is better. However, I believe that the current NHS system is extremely bloated in England, and it is facing a financial crisis, so it would seem that if such a system was instituted in the United States of America, it would be a disaster, as the national debt will increase substantially. So, this would mean that the national debt would have to decrease first in the United States of America, but then

---

[18] NHS Choices, NHS in England - help with health costs, http://www.nhs.uk/NHSEngland/Healthcosts/Pages/Prescriptioncosts.aspx.

[19] Ibid

[20] Ibid

before universal health care is offered, there must also be a very sizable surplus, while also instituting a new tax just to cover it. On the other hand, we must not let any politician institute such a program in the United States of America, as they would potentially drive up the national deficit and ruin health care for everyone, just like the Democrats and the Far Left did when they passed and implemented the Affordable Care Act. So, be careful of what you want, because universal health care can and has put some countries in a very deep financial deficit.

Well wait, there's more, as you have heard Trump, as some believe, has praised Australia's universal health care system during his attendance at a formal event. Well, Trump might have praised the health care system of Australia, but that does not mean anything, as he could have just been complimenting the current prime minister of the continent of Australia. In Australia, the universal health care system is known as Medicare, and it covers all costs related to public hospital treatment as well as subsidized and or free medical treatment by practitioners of medicine to all citizens and legal permanent residents of Australia.[21] Now, with regard to medicine to those eligible, it is mostly subsidized if you decide to become a member of

---

[21] ISelect, Medicare, http://www.iselect.com.au/overseas-visitors-cover/australian-health-system/medicare/.

the pharmaceutical benefits scheme, but if you don't have PBS then your medicine will be much more expensive.[22]

With Medicare, prescription medication is much lower and you are entitled to free health care if you are a patient of a government-run (public) hospital.[23] Now, people can also purchase private health insurance, and any eligible person could be entitled to an insurance rebate, which will not be discussed in this book.[24] But, with Medicare, if you are an eligible resident of Australia you might be entitled to reduced care costs in other countries when you visit, as there are reciprocal agreements existing between certain countries, yet when you need these reciprocal services it is usually reserved just for essential services and treatment.[25]

Now, as a precaution, just to receive Medicare benefits, you must register your local Australian bank account, if you are eligible for Medicare services.[26] But, when a health professional decides to bill you there are two ways: bulk billing by using the Medicare benefit as the full payment or using a patient account to directly charge you

---

[22] Australian Department of Human Services, Pharmaceutical Benefits Scheme, https://www.humanservices.gov.au/customer/services/medicare/pharmaceutical-benefits-scheme.

[23] Australian Department of Human Services, Medicare services, https://www.humanservices.gov.au/customer/subjects/medicare-services.

[24] Ibid

[25] Ibid

[26] Ibid

with a bill.[27] Yet, with a patient account, if you are an eligible resident, you may also claim or demand Medicare benefits be used to pay the medical doctor.[28] On the other hand, if you a visitor to Australia, you might be eligible to have subsidized health care in Australia if you are from Malta, Belgium, Finland, Ireland, Italy, the Netherlands, Slovenia, United Kingdom, Norway, New Zealand, and Sweden.[29] Now, here is where it gets complicated with subsidized Medicare services to visitors from certain eligible countries. If you are from Finland, Ireland, Norway, the United Kingdom, Sweden, and New Zealand, then you are completely covered, provided that you are a legal resident of one of those countries and currently have a valid visa.[30] If you are from Belgium, Slovenia, and or the Netherlands, you must have a valid European health insurance card in order to enroll, and you will have subsidized health care for as long as your legally authorized visit to Australia or until your European health insurance card expires.[31] Nevertheless, if you are a visitor from Malta and or Italy and are considered a legal and authorized resident or citizen of any of those two countries, then you will have subsidized health care in Australia for six months and no longer than that specific period of

---

[27] Ibid

[28] Ibid

[29] Australian Department of Human Services, Health care for visitors to Australia, https://www.humanservices.gov.au/customer/enablers/health-care-visitors-australia.

[30] Ibid

[31] Ibid

authorized time.[32] As a result, it seems confusing and complicated for specific outside visitors, but the Australian Medicare system is not that complicated once you get to know it.

With regard to universal health care, Canada, England, and Australia all have different and unique systems. But, not every system is the same. As we have heard from Bernie Sanders and other Socialists, they support all of these systems, even if they never evaluated them, as they believe health care is a right. Well, in the United States of America, health care is not a right, as all of our rights are from God, and besides, the founders and framers would not want government to run your lives because they tend to want a more effective system with very limited government involved. Personally, the three countries that offer some form of universal health care described in this book might look good and provide effective care, they tend to fall short of what the Socialists are saying about those systems. I believe that the Socialists who demand universal health care in the United States of America are just overplaying or overexaggerating the systems as a whole, because they just want to claim it is fine for everyone.

In reality, these universal health care systems have major flaws, and the Socialists fail to take them into account, because they just think the government will solve all of their problems.

---

[32] Ibid

Chapter Two

Culture, Free Speech, and Liberal Lunacy

T he image of culture can be described as a very

important issue for the majority of citizens and legal residents of the United States of America and other nations. However, Democrats and people who align themselves as being as part of the Political Left or Political Far Left of the Political Spectrum, have recently and for years has threw temper tantrums and mental breakdowns. The reason why the Democrats and the Far Left have these mental meltdowns and temper tantrums is due to they only support the "free speech" that they agree with. In other words, if you say something they don't like, then they will start getting angry by having mental breakdowns or throwing temper tantrums. So, it seems that anything these Far Left people disagree with, they will say is not free speech, as they consider it hate speech. The reason these Far Left people call free speech a form of hate speech is simply because they do not agree with it.

You see, the people of the Far Left, when they don't agree with what you say, well they will attempt to shut you down, because they believe their form of free speech is better and more superior to any other forms of free speech. The problems that the Democrats and the Far Left have are with that of conservatism, republicanism, and libertarianism. However, not every Democrat is part of the Far Left. The people who are part of the Far Left usually support some form or another of socialism, communism, and or Marxism, while also voicing their support for fascism and anarchism. The Far Left claims that they are part of the Anti-Fascist movement, but they are actually part of the Fascist movement, because they commit and engage in very violent and aggressive acts. Remember, fascism and anarchism openly supports the ideology that you need to be engaging in violent, aggressive, and criminal acts to get your point across. Well, even though they claim they hate Fascism, the Far Left has engaged in the act of fascism themselves, because they believe the other side is the enemy. As with their support and engagement of fascism, the Far Left actually engages in extremely violent acts, and they also engage in explosive riots and other criminal acts, yet they don't believe they are violent because they need to be violent in order to eradicate the people they don't agree with. Well, what we call this is hypocrisy, because it is actually the Far Left who supports and engages in fascism and anarchism, as they are violent, even though they claim that conservatives and republicans support fascism and anarchy. However, they just don't understand, as they know what they are doing is wrong, but they say they must do this because the other side is bad.

Well, the majority of conservatives and Republicans do not engage in violent protests (riots), arson, criminal acts, violence, or anything else illegal. No, instead, the conservatives and the Republicans engage in peaceful engagements and talks. The Democrats and the members of the Far Left, when they are upset at the political outcomes, they decide to act in an irrational manner that often leads them to riot, commit violence and violent acts, commit criminal acts, and act in a very aggressive manner that is often violent in nature. However, since the Democrats and the Far Left has such utter distaste, contempt, and hatred for anyone who disagrees with their views, conservatism, and republicans, they tend to manipulate everything as they see fit. So, it seems the Democrats and the Far Left want to falsify their evidence in order to fit their narrative as a whole. Here is the actual problem with the Democrats and the Far Left in today's modern society, they label fascism as "an authoritarian and nationalistic right-wing system of government and social organization."[33] Further, the general use definition of fascism has been redefined as, "extreme right-wing, authoritarian, or intolerant views or practice."[34] Not only is this offensive to the true meaning, but it is also wrong and misguided on so many levels of contempt. The true meaning of fascism is currently what is happening to the opposition in the country of Venezuela due to Maduro trying to obstruct everything with his narrative; and to coin the term of fascism even more, the people who are trying to delegitimize the election of Donald Trump while openly support public riots, violence, obstruct free speech, and engage in criminal acts are actually the fascisms themselves because they want to engage in obstructionist tactics that oppresses the opposition. So, what does this means as it relates to fascism, well it means that the Democrats and the Far Left hate conservatives and Republicans.

In fact, nowhere in the constitution does it say that governments of the states should adopt communist, socialist, Far Left, Democratic, and or extremist/authoritarianism forms of governments. The text of the constitution does indicate that "The United States shall guarantee to every State in this Union a Republican Form of Government, and shall protect each of them against Invasion; and on Application of the Legislature, or of the Executive (when the Legislature cannot be convened), against

---

[33] Derek Hunter, Google Redefines The Word 'Fascism' To Smear Conservatives, Protect Liberal Rioters, *Daily Caller*, February 4, 2017, http://dailycaller.com/2017/02/04/google-redefines-the-word-fascism-to-smear-conservatives-protect-liberal-rioters/.

[34] Ibid

domestic Violence.[35] So, what does this Republican form of government mean, well it means that government must be Republican in nature, as the founders and framers were very clear in their wording, since they feared that too much government control over anything would lead to an abuse of power. Of course, to the Democrats and the Far Left, the term of Republican is foreign to them, as they have complete disregard for the constitution, because they want to eliminate the opposition.

You see the Democrats and the members of the Far Left wants to always distort the truth when they see it necessary and fit, as this is usually due to their biased and irrational views of promoting fear and terror to scare people. For the Democrats and the Far Left, facts do not simply matter to them, and when someone gives them the facts, then those Democrats and the Far Left will attempt to discredit those facts, as they know they have lost the battle but continue to insist that their narrative is an alternative and better than the truth. The real meaning and or definition of fascism can be described as the following, "a political philosophy, movement, or regime (such as that of the Fascisti) that exalts nation and often race above the individual and that stands for a centralized autocratic government headed by a dictatorial leader, severe economic and social regimentation, and forcible suppression of opposition."[36]

---

[35] Heritage Foundation, Guarantee Clause, http://www.heritage.org/constitution/#!/articles/4/essays/128/guarantee-clause.

[36] Merriam-Webster, Definition of Fascism, https://www.merriam-webster.com/dictionary/fascism.

Further, fascism can also be described as, "a tendency toward or actual exercise of strong autocratic or dictatorial control."[37] The first meaning or definition of fascism is usually capitalized,[38] but it does not really matter how you spell and or punctuate it, because a fascist will always believe in fascism. To make a point clear it, the Democrats and the Far Left have abused the meaning of the word 'fascism," as they have knowingly left stuff out, since they want to label any right-winger a fascist. The reason why the Democrats want to label every single conservative and Republican a fascist is because the Democrats and the Far Left do not support the true ideologies of the constitution and the declaration of independence. The true intention of these Democrats and Far Left people is to promote hatred and hostility towards freedom, liberty, and peace. You think the Democrats and the Far Left has learned by now, but they continue to spew their false facts and their propaganda. When they say something and it is proven to be false, as it always is, it is propaganda, because they want to create and then maintain a movement based upon false pretenses. These pretenses do not exist because they are manufactured by people who have nothing better to do than lie.

Remember that real definition of fascism that I just discussed, well it seems that the Democrats and Far Left who hate conservatives and Republicans do not like that real definition, as they want to make their own up that fits their own perspective political views. So, it

---

[37] Ibid

[38] Ibid

seems that nothing is as it is seen. The conservatives and Republicans who support a limited government ideology do not meet the real meaning of believing in fascism or being a fascist. In fact, in order to meet the definition of being a fascist and or believing in fascism, one must meet all the criteria mentioned. So, you tell this to someone who is a Democrat and or a member of the Far Left, well they will attempt to attack you based on their hatred. The point that the Democrats and the Far Left wants to make is that every other narrative is inferior to theirs, since they believe the truth does not matter. They constantly spew their hate towards anyone they disagree with, even to members of their own belief, political party, creed, political faction, and other similar qualities. You think they would agree with people who are part of their own political party or political faction, but that is not what happens, as the Democrats and the Far Left has a certain ideology that demands that all should be entitled. Yep, that's right; their argument is that entitlements should exist for everyone, even though you might not deserve it. For one, this reasoning is misguided and wrong, since you must work hard in order to earn something, and most reasonable people will tell you will need to work hard in order to earn it. However, these Democrats and the members of the Far Left see it otherwise. They don't care if you worked for it or not, as they believe everyone should get a piece of the pie or cake. This has and always will be a tactic of the Democrats and the Far Left, as they knew why they lost, but they still don't accept it. It is the reason why they will never understand why people of other political beliefs have different opinions than them. There is nothing wrong with having differing political opinions; but the Democrats and the Far Left only believe there is one correct type of political view, which is that conservatives and Republicans must be silenced because we don't agree with them. Now, this type of shutting down is not new, as it is a common view amongst the Democrats and the members of the Far Left who refuse to accept opposing views, political or not. It is a disease that should be considered a detriment to society, as the meaning to oppose debate of different opinions amounts to fascism as a whole, and this in turn does nothing good for the rest of society. Well, the Political Left does not believe in other people's opinion, as they know they will lose the debate.

The purpose of this silencing is that the Political Left only wants to tell and believe their biased narrative. Now, as stated, the Political Left is a bunch of hypocrites, since they understand nothing but their facts. These facts that the Political Left are trying to portray are actually opinions, as most of them have no respect for a conservative or Republican, even if they claim they are open to all political beliefs. Yet, in reality, they have nothing better to do than complain, because they have no patience, so they start riots that encourages and promotes violence, criminal acts, and aggression. The fact of the matter is that this type of behavior does nothing to solve the problem of hate, because the goal of the Political Left is to spread hate and fear across the World and the United States of America. We must unite, but they will not unite in the correct way, since their way of uniting is to destruct and oppose the ideas of everyone they don't agree with. It is confusing, as you might see, but when you have a firsthand account of what these people constantly do; well, it is something that puzzles many people, except for the Political Left. However, there is something that is crazy about the Political Left, and that is because they tend to accept everything you say, or so you thought.

Well, what have we here? We have here that the Political Left is and always will be the promoters of free speech and expression for any person who expresses it. It is that what is so concerning, because the Political Left promotes nothing of that sort, unless they agree with that type of speech. Under the Political Left, the only freedom of speech and expression they promote is the basis of inclusion, which might seem as a legitimate concern, but they are definitely supporting inclusion, since they promote intolerance. Well, you thought they promoted inclusion, well you were told wrong. The form of inclusion the Political Left openly supports and engages in is in the form of isolating anyone who has a different opinion or political viewpoint. So, that does not seem like inclusion, because it is not inclusion. This kind of inclusion that they openly promote and believe in only supports the idea that everyone should have the same political beliefs and opinions as them. Indeed, this means if you are a conservative or a Republican, you will be attacked based simply on your own opinions. That isn't inclusion, because that is the promotion as a form of fascism and fascist ideology. This claim of inclusion will not hold up to the truth, but they say it does, even though they know it promotes fascism and anarchy. The promotion of fascism is nothing new, but they must take responsibility, and yet they don't because they believe everyone they agree with is fascist and supports fascism. In fact, they are intentionally misleading the true meaning of fascism, as they are scared of the truth.

This promoting of inclusion is misguided, and is tantamount to fraud, because the promotion of the use of inclusion by the Political Left is flawed and biased, since it is based on their own narrative. For one thing, they do not care about their beliefs, as they believe it is their goal to prevent other forms of freedom of expression. So, to put it into their own words, the Political Left only supports the idea of inclusion for everyone and anyone if they agree with your political opinions and views. Quite puzzling, isn't it. Well, this is the same thing as they claim to promote tolerance for all. You see, the Political Left says that they promote tolerance, but in fact they promote intolerance because they hate you if you have a different political view or opinion. This in fact is hypocrisy, as they clearly do not support tolerance, since they only support free speech they agree with. If you have a different political opinion, the Political Left will demand that your freedom of speech and or expression be shut down because it promotes racism, sexism, bigotry, xenophobia, Islamophobia, or other forms of alleged hatred. Now, we all know that this use of political name calling is just an excuse because the Political Left hates other political opinions and beliefs. They will attempt to do anything to shut you down.

Now, it is a fact that they promote intolerance and exclusion, as the Political Left only supports their own political ideology that they agree with. They will stop at all costs, and they might even punch you to prove something, since their only goal is to stop anyone who has an opposing political ideology. This ideology, as expected, is rooted in the area of craziness. There is nothing else that can convince them because they are too ignorant. So, what is this all about anyway, well the answer might not surprise you, as the reason is to promote their flawed agenda. Their topic and action plan is to promote tolerance and inclusion, which you have already heard, but what is their focus on this action plan, well you will find out soon, which is now. The idea of promoting tolerance is to accept everyone, no matter their beliefs, values, and or opinions, whether it involves politics or is apolitical. Now, let's take a look at the tolerance that the Democrats and the Far Left accepts. The Democrats and the Far Left only supports tolerance if it meets their ideology, such as if it is in line with their political opinions. Now, we know that the beliefs, views, values, and political opinions of the Political Left are extremely flawed, if not mentioned before, but their form of the term tolerance is if it is the same as theirs. So what does this mean, well it means that opposing views do not matter to the Political Left. If you say something to them that they don't agree with, they will call it hate speech, even though it is not hate speech. Now, you thought they were very accepting, yet the Political Left only accepts their own opinions. So, this means that anything else is not factual to them, and they believe you are inciting hate against them.

The Political Left is triggered that you said something they do not agree with, and this is what they call a micro aggression. The

Political Left does not care what other people think, because they only care about themselves. It is a matter of their biased and bigoted ways of not accepting the truth and or other opinions. But, of course, the Far Left and the Democrats will tell you they are not bigoted because they support the ideology of inclusion and tolerance. This concept of bigotry seems foreign to them, as they claim they have no hate for anyone and or anything. Now, the Political Left will always say that they are always very accepting and tolerant of everyone, no matter what the differences are. Bigotry, to the Political Left, is what they use against people who have different views, values, opinions, and beliefs than them. So, you see, the Political Left cites that you are a bigot if you just have a different opinion. Now you see that the Democrats and the Far Left are not so tolerant or accepting as they say they are, since they start openly attacking people with different opinions, views, beliefs, and or values. But, when questioned about this behavior of attacking people who hold differences of opinions, values, beliefs, and views, they say it is necessary to stop the hatred and promotion of fascism. Well, now you have them saying that they like and embrace tolerance, inclusion, and differences, but now they are acting like hypocrites because they are actually against inclusion and tolerance.

This behavior of accepting everyone by being tolerant and inclusive and then acting in an intolerant and non-inclusive manner is tantamount to hypocrisy, as stated before. Nothing should surprise you about the Political Left or their hypocritical behavior of saying they are accepting of everyone. It is a tactic they use just to complain about their problems with people having different opinions, values, views, and beliefs. Their intolerance is amazing, isn't it, well; it should not be a surprise to you, as they have always been this way. They never ceased to amaze you, and they only are tolerant of people who are expressing the same feelings and opinions of them. It is simply amazing how they like to spin their narrative of treating everyone with dignity and respect, but the Political Left is never dignified and always acts disrespectful towards people they don't agree with. Interesting, isn't it, well don't be surprised, as you will continue the Political Left to use this type of hypocritical behavior.

Suggesting that the Political Left accepts people of every origin, race, creed, ethnicity, and nationality is not an understatement but it is also not an overstatement. They do accept people who are different than them, but when you suddenly become or are a conservative or part of the Republican Party, well the Political Left starts to attack you. Even though you disagree with the Political Left and are in the less Radical Left, you are still demonized for spreading hatred. The Political Left members of their own political party and factions, because they believe certain members must express the same feelings, beliefs, views, and values as everyone else in their factions.

This fake narrative of the Political Left is starting to get somewhat ridiculous, but they don't care. The Political Left rather wants to protest conservative, libertarian, and Republican speakers for not being like them. Simply for being a member of a different political party or not having the same political beliefs and opinions will make you a target of the Political Left. It is noteworthy that the Political Left has an opinion, but at what expense does it become dangerous and extremely inappropriate. The answer is when they actually threaten people. You see, the Political Left has this belief that it is fine and dandy to attack people with different political perspectives; well, when you present it that way, the Political Left has now broken their rule of acceptance, inclusion, and tolerance. The Political Left demonizes everything they see as pro-capitalist, conservative, libertarian and Republican in nature, because they don't believe in those political views. The Political Left calls free speech from other political beliefs hate speech and fascism, as they have nothing better else to do.

Demonizing is something that is well-regarded in the Political Left community, as it is meant to use disinformation to oppose the views of everyone who is conservative, Republican, and or libertarian in nature. Sure, it is simple, but they hold riots and protests where speakers are holding their events. Now, these public events are meant to tell the attendees about why they probably should support freedom and liberty, but these events might also explain why it is important to stand up for your own rights. However, the Political Left does not want you to know that, as they believe that being a conservative, a libertarian, or being a Republican is the same as hate speech. The true intention of these events held on school campuses is to promote freedom of expression, freedom of speech, liberty, and an open dialogue that promotes an open debate of how the information might be relevant to a person's life. The events held by conservative and Republican speakers at schools are meant to promote nothing but honesty about how bad socialism and communism is. These events are meant to promote freedom of the press and to express unity. But, then there is dissent, and it is from the Political Left, in the form of not dissent, but of violence and engaging in criminal and aggressive acts. So, there you have it, the dissent of the Political Left is oppression and suppressing different political beliefs, as they believe any conservative, libertarian, and Republican is the same as supporting fascism. Being a conservative, a libertarian, and or part of the Republican Party is not the promotion of fascism, as those three right-wing ideologies of conservatism, libertarianism, and Republicanism is the promotion of free speech, limited government, freedom of the press, liberty, and freedom.

Now, the Political Left claims hate speech is not covered by the constitution of the United States of America; well, they are wrong, because in the United States of America you can express and say anything you want, no matter how hurtful or untrue it might actually be. The reason the Political Left says this is that they believe all free speech by conservatives, libertarians, and or Republicans is a form of hate speech. Hate speech, no matter how divisive, is still protected by the constitution. However, speech that is not covered and is considered to be illegal and or unconstitutional is that of threatening people in order to harm them, such as when a person claims they are going to kill people in order to promote terrorism. Promoting and openly supporting any form of illegal behavior is illegal and is not covered by the constitution, so people should choose their words wisely. Now, what else type of speech is not covered, well other types of speech that are not protected is promoting violence, promoting criminal behavior, and or promoting anything that is illegal. When the Political Left says something is hate speech, it is not usually illegal; as the majority of the time, hate speech is actually legal and constitutionally protected by and in the Bill of Rights of the constitution of the United States of America. Often, the Political Left will call any type of legally and constitutionally protected free speech from conservatives and Republicans hate speech, only because the Political Left does not agree with it. It is in fact not hate speech, but the Political Left now likes to call everything hate speech when a conservative and or Republican says anything. So, the problem is that you have the Political Left as the opposition, calling it hate speech, when really it is not. The Political Left likes to claim everything said by a conservative and or Republican is hate speech, since it does not represent the same values as the Political Left. It is simply a stated tactic, as probably stated before.

Everything to the Political Left is considered racist, sexist, bigotry, xenophobic, Islamaphobic, and misogynist, if it originates from a conservative and or a Republican. Now, the Political Left adds in a new term, which is fascism. The true meanings and definitions of fascism have already been stated, but the Political Left would like to ignore that and make up their own meaning or definition. Simply put, the antifascists are actually fascists, as their main goal is to resist and oppose everything they don't agree with. And then, there is the act of anarchy, which actually promotes violence, as well as engaging in it, just to promote their ideology of opposition, resistance, and violence. You would think the Political Left is ashamed of their actions, but they openly encourage it, as that is the only thing that they can focus on. It is rather sad for the Political Left, but opposition, resistance, violence, and committing criminal and aggressive acts are the goals of an antifascist, where the antifascists actually support fascism because they openly are seen engaging in it. This is nothing new, but this type of political ideology started to develop in a worse manner when Trump was elected, and that is because the Obama administration had a distaste for the law enforcement community as well as having a distaste for the constitution and showing support for radical terrorist groups such as the Black Panthers, Black Lives Matter, and the Muslim Brotherhood, and for also overthrowing legitimate and well-governed governments. Now, the Political Left will try to dispute this, but many of them support nation building, and in nation building, the nation who changes the government of the foreign country puts in someone far worse than you have ever thought in your life, but we will not get into that here, but we will discuss culture later.

Anyways, it is fine to express your own free speech, but it is considered illegal and unconstitutional to infringe on and or to prevent free speech rights of other people. The Political Left is guilty of doing and or committing this act of infringing on free speech, as they continue to successfully block or to cancel speaking events of conservatives and or Republicans on college campuses. Now, the Political Left infringes on free speech by making it unsafe for the speakers to hold their private and or sponsored events. But the Political Left believes it is necessary to infringe on other peoples' rights in order to make a statement just because the other people are conservative or Republican, and to the Political Left a conservative or Republican is considered an automatic fascist. Isn't that nice; just because you have a different political ideology you are considered a fascist automatically. Well, the reasoning behind the Political Left automatically naming a conservative and or any Republican a fascist is because the Political Left does not agree with being a conservative and or a Republican. So, the Political Left will always label you a fascist automatically if you are either a Republican or a conservative just because you might not agree with them. This thinking and reasoning of the Political Left is just ridiculous and makes them unserious about their life choices.

One thing about the Political Left is that when making their outlandish and untrue statements about conservatives and Republicans is that they actually believe their own propaganda, well most of the time. And this propaganda normally consists of disputed statements but mostly they just believe everyone who disagrees with them is a fascist because that is all they can think of. In other words, the Political Left makes up a lame excuse because they can't think of anything else, so it would seem nothing matters to them. Yes, of course that is the action plan they seek, because the Political Left is void of truth, and the only thing that they have left is to attack someone they don't agree with. You see, the Political Left wants everyone to be the same and act like them, so you now basically understand now that if you are not the same it means you are not welcome. The Political Left is strange and are hypocrites, while also not caring about what could happen to them, because they believe violence, criminal acts, and riots are necessary. It is a case of extreme anarchy, but they say otherwise, as the Political Left wants to make an excuse for everything that they did wrong. So, if someone from the Political Left commits a crime, such as arson or using violence and aggression to beat up another person, then they will face some sort of punishment. Well, you could be right, as what that particular member did was an actual crime(s), but you are probably wrong as well. The reason why you might be wrong is that when the Political Left holds their allegedly nonviolent and peaceful protests, they are not held accountable for their actions; as many times when they allegedly hold their riots, they are in a place that actually promotes the ideals of Leftist propaganda. You now have speaking events that are boycotted by the Political Left because of the speaker's political ideology, and so the Political Left shows up in force to commit all sorts of crimes and riots because they do not like the speaker. They curse, they name call based on political reasons, and they demand that everyone be treated with respect. Well, the problem with the Political Left's demands is that they do not make sense, because it is actually the Political Left who does not respect anyone. The Political Left only respects their standings and opinions, which simply means they will only respect something that they agree with. If the Political Left does not agree with what you say, then they will riot and commit crimes, but it doesn't end there. You see, if the Political Left does not like a specific policy, they will demand change, which simply equates to nothing more than entitlements for the minorities. You see, the Political Left wants everything to be free and they also believe any minority race and or ethnicity need to replace the race/ethnicity of the majority. Well, there isn't really a race/ethnicity of majority, as many are of European ancestry and not every European person is Caucasian. Well now, the problem with the Political Left is that they hate White People, as they constantly blame the White People for everything, and so they believe the White People must be replaced by minorities.

Never mind about inclusion, because they want to erase history as we know it; and by simply excluding a certain race of people, the Political Left is actually exclusive, as they want to exclude certain people. But, not everything is as you see, yet when you come back to the possible consequences for the Political Left, you will see that the police are either forced to stand down by other members of the Political Left or choose not to engage in deescalating the riots and crimes being committed by the Political Left, and this is nothing new. To put this problem of the Political Left in perspective, they have a complaining and whining for entitlements problems, as they believe everything should be theirs without them earning it. Sure, they favor entitlements, but the Political Left also demands diversity training for everyone, because they want everyone to feel sensitive about other peoples' feelings. Well, in the real world, everything is serious, and you can't always say you are sorry. No, in the real world you need to work hard in order to earn something, but the Political Left still does not care and understand. The Political Left demands diversity training because they feel that certain people are too sensitive to handle a certain situation, but in actuality these overly sensitive people can't succeed in life if they always complain about everything. The fact that diversity training is mandated by some people and organizations is the reason why the United States of America and many other countries are giving away their sovereignty and their original cultural heritage.

Well now, culture you say, that is supposed to be a very off-limits and controversial topic. Well, here is the problem with the topic of discussing culture. The Political Left has hijacked the culture narrative in order to manipulate how culture and cultural heritage should be treated and or handled. The Political Left is trying to undermine the cultural heritage of the United States of America, even though certain areas of history might be sensitive or outrageous to some people. On the other hand, it is generally known that people do not support the aspect and or ideology of slavery, but that aspect or ideology of not supporting slavery is not shared around the world, as certain workers in specific areas of the world are part of the slave trade. Now, slavery is usually illegal, but people try to get around it by being creative about the law, but the traffickers also hide and try to outsmart everyone who is after them. Slavery should be condemned, as it is considered illegal, but it also deprives the victims of a normal life. Modern slavery as you know it can consist of anything, such as manual labor to high-end prostitution. In the aspect of high-end prostitution, it is basically also commonly known or referred to as sexual and human trafficking. As for the manual labor aspect, this type of slavery usually involves children in the cocoa labor distribution. Children are the actual slaves in the case of manual labor, as children are trafficked in order to become manual laborers in the chocolate production industry. The child manual labor slave industry usually occurs in places where cocoa is harvested and processed, so in other words, this exists in many poor parts of the world, but where there are forests, rainforests, and the woods.

Now, why doesn't the Political Left complain about children being forced to harvest and process cocoa? Well, maybe it's because they like chocolate, or it could be they just don't know. But, the real reason is that the Political Left is too preoccupied of helping with outrageous social justice issues. So, why is social justice so important, because it promotes their ideology of nothing but intolerance? These social justice issues are just ridiculous, as the goal of the Political Left is to make everyone the same. In other words, the Political Left wants to make sure you are indoctrinated with their views. It is common for these social justice warriors to criticize anything they don't agree with. These social justice warriors are a major part of the Political Left and their goal to undermine the values and respect for laws. Instead, these social justice warriors are just rioters and violent protesters who demand that the history of the world needs to be changed because of racism. The reason why these social justice warriors demand history be removed is because they don't like it; and so, instead, these social justice warriors demand that history needs to change because of how they view the world. The focus of the social justice warriors is to disregard any human history that they don't agree with. It is the belief of the social justice warriors that they are being mistreated; well, the social justice warriors are essentially wrong because they are actually living in their own bubble. This simply means that the social justice warriors and the Political Left cannot handle the truth. The Political Left and the social justice warriors don't want to accept the truth because they don't want to believe it; and so they decide to wage often violent protests that lead to rioting and criminal acts, as well as people being arrested. These social justice warriors often take the name of being antifascists, but they are not antifascists, since they are actually out in force in order to oppose the people they disagree with. They constantly complain that they are being mistreated, but their complaints are just frivolous. The only time when the complaints are not frivolous and insane is when an actual injustice actually occurs. And while actual injustices do occur, such as being wrongfully jailed or imprisoned, the social justice warriors and the Political Left want to make everything a social injustice. So, you see why their complaints are insane, as the Political Left and the social justice warriors only want to seek attention. It is a sad case of not knowing the truth while also demonizing the system. While the system is flawed and imperfect, the social justice warriors and the Political Left wants to change the rules of society so that they can benefit by simply imposing a mandate of diversity training on everyone.

Ah, diversity training, which demands you to think carefully about what you say to other people, well diversity training mandates that some people are too sensitive to everything, and because of that you must not speak that way or say a particular statement, word, and or phrase that might trigger that specific person to become angry, upset, and or saddened. Well, the truth is that overly sensitive people need to just deal with it, as the majority of the stuff they hear that triggers them is actually not offensive. The overly sensitive people are only easily offended of what was said is because of their nativity of the subject as well as being misinformed about everything they hear and see. It is essentially a matter that they don't want to hear anything they don't agree with, as it triggers them. You will hear the Political Left and their social justice warrior faction that they are mistreated, and because of that mistreatment they are going to unlawfully take over the streets, rooms, buildings, and other places were events might be held. They complain that no one cares about them, but in reality they do not respect the laws of the land. It is a term that is known as political correctness, as the social justice warriors and the Political Left believe everyone should be politically correct because certain people are too sensitive. Well, in the real world, you can't always complain, as you must work hard, but you will also need to work with people who might disagree with you. So, a complaint that they make that people don't care about them is very inaccurate, as they always their parents, family, and or friends to spoon-feed them with comfort because of hurt feelings. These overly sensitive people need to get over themselves, as life isn't a safe space, as it is a place with diversity.

The diversity that the Political Left and the so-called social justice warriors seek, as their meaning of diversity is to limit public and private opinion of everything and anything. They demand a safe space to be comforted by their friends and other people, as they are too overly sensitive about what they hear. So, in the end, they demand change, but this change is a mandate that demands everyone takes diversity training and or sensitivity training. There is no difference between these two types of training, as they focus on the same ideology: mandating a change in behavior. But, sensitivity training is usually described by people as not saying offensive words to people, and what they call is offensive is usually not considered offensive. On the other hand, what is known as diversity training is simply is something that demands you to change your behavior because of race/ethnicity relations. In other words, people describe diversity training as something that promotes a better understanding of the different races, cultures, and ethnicities around the world. The added focus of diversity training simply means that everyone is diverse, but both diversity training and sensitivity training are about the same. Again, the role of these two types of training are actually universally similar, as diversity focuses on cultural awareness while sensitivity focuses on everything, so it seems nothing is more supported than mandatory brainwashing.

Ah, yes, brainwashing, something that is frowned upon by mostly everyone, but actually not condemned by the Political Left, as the Political Left demands you change your views if they do not like and or agree with your beliefs and or opinions. By just being a conservative and or Republican and you say something publicly or privately, some social justice warrior or the Political Left will find what you said is offensive. Now, the reason why the social justice warriors or Political Left find your statements offensive is that they will never agree with you, as the social justice warriors and the Political Left are living in their own fantasy land where they believe everything should be a safe space and that no one should ever face criticism. To put it simply into context, the Political Left and the social justice warriors faction wants to silence you if you identify as a conservative, a libertarian (conservative), and or as a Republican. They have to respect for order and they keep on breaking it, so you might say that they are just thugs. Nevertheless, the rise of the so-called social justice warrior faction is just a façade, as they really don't like anything, even if it is part of the Political Left agenda. Yet, the social justice warrior faction should be classified as being part of the Alt Left because of their views being extreme. At the same time, the Political Left should also be classified as being part of the Alt Left because their views are also extreme. The Political Left have long departed that of the True Left, with the True Left consisting of conservative and moderate Democrats, but the Political Left does not care because they support and demand entitlements and Marxism. Well, it also seems that the majority or all of the social justice warriors are just psychotic and anti-social people because they just refuse to follow the norms and the standards of society. In other words, the social justice warriors will refuse to follow the laws and regulations of society because they don't believe in any of them, as they see laws and regulations as part of the problem.

To give examples of what a social justice warrior might demand, well there are certainly many atrocious examples. In one instance, one social justice warrior demanded that all white people give up their money and belongings to the black and indigenous people as a form of repatriation.[39] So, that social justice warrior clearly hates white people and so she demands that all white people give up everything they have because she believes it belongs to the black and indigenous people;[40] well, what that social refuses to recognize is that did those black and indigenous people actually work for that. Basically, this social justice warrior is just demanding entitlements for people who probably never earned them. But then, this social justice warrior also demands there be killings, yet is described as being a pre-school teacher.[41] However, the most startling statement she makes is that she knows the money belongs to the white people but she is the person who actually wants that money in order to benefit her own name.[42] To put it into context, this social justice warrior hates white people, and it is a clear sign she is completely full of herself and is a real racist; and at the same time, this social justice warrior hates capitalism and has threatened the

---

[39] Tyler Durden, "Seattle Social Justice Warrior Demands 'Reparations' Or "We Need To Start Killing People...," *Zero Hedge*, February 2, 2017, http://www.zerohedge.com/news/2017-02-01/seattle-social-justice-warrior-demands-reparations-or-we-need-start-killing-people.

[40] Ibid

[41] Ibid

[42] Ibid

White House.[43] At the same time, this social justice warrior claims that capitalism is racism while also using profanity throughout her rant; yet, she demands she is entitled to other peoples' money because she just does not like white people as a whole.[44]

Yet, in another claim, social justice warriors at the University of Michigan demand that black people have their own segregated space in order to allegedly work on social justice matters.[45] This demand from a student group is because the University of Michigan is currently in the process of building a multicultural center in the middle of the campus, and so these social justice warriors believe they are entitled to their own space because they don't want to share a space with people of European or Caucasian descent.[46] However, if you think that is crazy, wait until you learn about their views on cultural appropriation and food are. You will see that the social justice warriors have surely lost their minds, as they are just acting ridiculous and insane.

It is especially ridiculous on why every one of those social justice warriors is acting irrational, insane, and in an incoherent manner. These social justice warriors think they are helping the world but in fact they are the cause for divisiveness and division. Besides

---

[43] Ibid

[44] Ibid

[45] Thomas Dishaw, "Social justice warriors demand 'segregated spaces' at University of Michigan," *News Target*, February 24, 2017, http://www.newstarget.com/2017-02-24-social-justice-warriors-demand-segregated-spaces-at-university-of-michigan.html.

[46] Ibid

that fact, these social justice warriors demand that if foreign food is served in the United States of America, that it should be served in its authentic and original manner. Well, someone needs to tell those social justice warriors that not every person makes it the same way as people from other regions. And, foreigners of course, such as an American, who make different cultural food (food from different countries), well that foreigner will have their own unique spin on the dish, yet will use only the types of ingredients that are available to them.

Take for example that the college dining hall at Oberlin College decided to make an Asian-inspired dish, in which the foreign-born students condemn that it is not authentic because of how it was made.[47] The problem that these foreign-born social justice warriors have with the food is that it was poorly made and or crafted when applied in a culturally-relevant manner.[48] Now, here is what the fuss it all about foreign-born social justice warriors complains about. They complain that the food is not ethnically correct. For example, one student from Vietnam was upset, angered, and or triggered that the Banh Mi sandwich was not up to standards because the pork was not grilled and there was a lack of ingredients that were included.[49] This

---

[47] Mitchell Blatt, "Social Justice Warriors At Oberlin Don't Know Anything About Ethnic Food," *The Federalist*, January 4, 2016, http://thefederalist.com/2016/01/04/social-justice-warriors-at-oberlin-dont-know-anything-about-ethnic-food/.

[48] Ibid

[49] Clover Linh Tran, "CDS Appropriates Asian Dishes, Students Say," *Oberlin Review*, November 6, 2015, http://oberlinreview.org/9055/news/cds-appropriates-asian-dishes-students-say/.

student from Vietnam was all upset that it did not have the same ingredients when crafted and or made in the country of Vietnam and proceeded to say that the food company in charge does not respect cuisines of Asian countries.[50] The student from Vietnam says that the recipe shows disrespect because it was modified; and so, the claim is that it should not be modified as the only way it should be made is the same way as in Vietnam.[51] So, what this foreign-born social justice warrior fails to understand is that people and companies are always trying to find out new ways to design and or to create recipes, as it adds a sense of creativity and elegance to the food item. However, the foreign-born social justice warriors complain that the real recipe has been manipulated in a gross manner and that the food item that is produced does not make it traditional and or authentic.[52] At the same time, the chaos and the ridiculousness does not end there, as now a foreign-born social justice warrior from China got angered that the version of General Tso's Chicken she ate was not authentic enough, as she stated her reasoning for being frustrated was that it was not actually fried but instead was steamed.[53] This is utterly ridiculous and insane, as the foreign-born social justice warrior found it strange and or weird that her potential meal was steamed, and further refused to taste the product because the sauce was a

---

[50] Ibid

[51] Ibid

[52] Ibid

[53] Ibid

substitution.[54] What did foreign-born social justice warrior does not know is that General Tso's Chicken is not an actual or authentic dish, as the Chinese people in China do not even make it; but instead, General Tso's Chicken was created by a person from China who then moved to Taiwan and then finally went to the United States of America to open up a famous restaurant in the city of New York.[55]

Even more, another restauranteur in the city of New York claims that his Chinese restaurant created General Tso's Chicken sometime in the past; yet, the person who first migrated from China stated that he intentionally altered the recipes for people who were not from the Hunanese province of China.[56] In fact, the people from the province of Hunan in China finds sweet and sugary foods as something that is foreign to them, meaning it does not make sense to their overall appetite.[57] Instead, the people from the Hunan province of China prefer their food to be flagrant and spicy, so it seems social justice warriors do not actually know their cultural heritage, as they fail to actually know and or understand the actual origins of food.[58] In fact, that sandwich that the foreign-born social justice warrior

---

[54] Ibid

[55]   Mitchell Blatt, "Social Justice Warriors At Oberlin Don't Know Anything About Ethnic Food," *The Federalist*, January 4, 2016, http://thefederalist.com/2016/01/04/social-justice-warriors-at-oberlin-dont-know-anything-about-ethnic-food/.

[56] Ibid

[57] Ibid

[58] Ibid

from Vietnam complained about was actually invented due to the French colonizing the country of Vietnam, so it seems this is further proof that these social justice warriors are clueless and or incompetent about their cultural heritage.[59] But, this food craziness does not end there, as there are also some insane social justice warriors who complain about sushi.

Now, this foreign-born social justice warrior from Japan does not like the Sushi prepared by the cafeteria because it is not prepared properly, saying that it is disrespect for the dish to be served because the rice is undercooked and the fish is not fresh enough and not much of a choice of fresh fish exists.[60] This foreign-born social justice warrior from Japan also makes a complaint about the sushi not being up to par because it can take several years to master the craft of making sushi as a whole; but, this social justice warrior also finds it offensive that food from cultures should not be modified, as if it is made by someone from another culture then it is not really authentic.[61] Yet, some foreign-born students are not complaining about the different types of cultural foods because they say the cafeteria is only using of what is available to them; so, it is fair to say that you need to substitute different ingredients if you don't have

---

[59] Ibid

[60] Clover Linh Tran, "CDS Appropriates Asian Dishes, Students Say," *Oberlin Review*, November 6, 2015, http://oberlinreview.org/9055/news/cds-appropriates-asian-dishes-students-say/.

[61] Ibid

access to the preferred ingredients.[62] Further, these foreign-born social justice warriors demand that their food be correct. In other words, the correct term for these social justice warriors is that they are considered to be gastronomically correct.[63] If you found that to be ridiculous and or insane, you are probably correct, as Oberlin College is the alma mater of Far Left actress Lena Dunham.[64] Now, you have not heard one of the most ridiculous and insane things that happened, which was that for some reason, the black student union decided to protest with the foreign-born social justice warriors at Oberlin College. You could say that these people who are part of the black student union are social justice warriors but they would properly classify themselves as being members of Black Lives Matter; yet, you could also say that these black students decided to protest because they claim that Black American recipes don't contain many recipes that use cream as an ingredient.[65] But, there were even more complaints about the food at Oberlin College and this time the complaints came from a Hindu-American association in Nevada because beef was used in the traditional Indian dish of tandoori.[66]

---

[62] Ibid

[63] Melkorka Licea and Laura Italiano, "Students at Lena Dunham's college offended by lack of fried chicken," *New York Post*, December 18, 2015, http://nypost.com/2015/12/18/pc-students-at-lena-dunhams-college-offended-by-lack-of-fried-chicken/.

[64] Ibid

[65] Ibid

[66] Ibid

Well, the fact of the matter is that many of the people who are part of the Hindu religion do not eat meat, but it is an attributed fact that many (millions of) Hindus do eat some form of meat such as beef and or buffalo.[67] Nevertheless, it is reported that only less than one percent of all Hindus eat beef and or buffalo, but there are different laws across the country of India, so some laws exists in certain regions that outlaws cow slaughtering.[68] However, whether you eat meat or not, that is not even insane as a social justice warrior that you not celebrate a holiday of different cultural heritage, as they claim that you should not be allowed to celebrate foreign traditions.

Now, take this story about a college student celebrating Cinco de Mayo, where a social justice warrior becomes upset that a white student is wearing a serape to celebrate the holiday.[69] Now, this social justice warrior demands that the student not celebrate Cinco de Mayo because he is not Mexican, and then further claims that he should not be celebrating the holiday because it is not his holiday.[70] In the video, this social justice apparently seems upset over a ridiculous and insane

---

[67] Omar Rashid and Ashok Kumar, "More Indians eating beef, buffalo meat," *The Hindu*, October 29, 2016, updated December 02, 2016, http://www.thehindu.com/news/national/%E2%80%98More-Indians-eating-beef-buffalo-meat%E2%80%99/article16085248.ece.

[68] Ibid

[69] Anthony Gockowski, "White student accosted for wearing serape on Cinco de Mayo," *Campus Reform*, May 09, 2017, https://www.campusreform.org/?ID=9158.

[70] Ibid

thing, that a white person is celebrating a Mexican holiday.[71] The social justice warrior is so upset that a white person is wearing a serape to celebrate a foreign holiday that she is triggered by it, treats it as a micro aggression, and then becomes offended that the student is not Mexican.[72] Then, the social justice warrior claims that the poncho is for people of Mexican culture and that the student is allegedly representing the culture of Mexico in a stereotypical manner.[73] Further, the social justice warrior claims that the student is being offensive to the Mexican culture because the social justice warrior is claiming that the student is portraying as all Mexicans of wearing a poncho and drink alcoholic beverages for a living (job or career).[74] The social justice warrior clearly does not understand what she is talking about because she only wants Mexicans to celebrate Cinco de Mayo, as described in the video, but this social justice warrior also claims that by dressing up in a poncho and celebrating the holiday the student is humiliating Mexicans around the world.[75] For no apparent reason, this social justice warrior is so offended that she does not believe a person of another culture should celebrate the culture and holidays of different cultures.

---

[71] Ibid

[72] Ibid

[73] Ibid

[74] Ibid

[75] Ibid

Further, it does not end there, as the social justice warrior actually wanted the university to intervene on her behalf, but then she also makes a diversity charge that the university is supposed to celebrate diversity.[76] Clearly, this social justice warrior does not identify the meaning of celebrating diversity, as when diversity is celebrated, it is meant for anyone who wants to participate in it. Sure, people of all cultures will celebrate anything diverse that is if they want to join in on the festivities. So, this social justice warrior believes that the student not of the Mexican should not celebrate the Mexican culture because it is against the pledge of diversity; well, the explanation of this social justice warrior clearly does not know the meaning of celebrating diversity.[77] It is clearly a ploy by the Political Left to become easily offended because they do not support what you are doing. At the same time, she believes it is demeaning and or offensive to the people of Mexico that non-Mexicans are actually celebrating Cinco de Mayo; but then this social justice warrior said she became disgusted and miserable because people of non-Mexican descent were celebrating Cinco de Mayo, while also calling it an attack against diversity.[78] However, that is probably not the most insane part of it. The social justice warrior then stated she felt so angered that people of non-Mexican heritage were celebrating Cinco de Mayo that she was unable to eat food on campus in the

---

[76] Ibid

[77] Ibid

[78] Ibid

university's dining halls.[79] Well, what we have here is a snowflake that is afraid of diversity, the real world, and of the truth, as it is common for a snowflake or a person who also complains about the real world in a constant manner that the world is unfair and misguided. So, what do these snowflakes do, well they always want to be comforted in some sort of safe space because they feel threatened by a non-threatening thing or event and because they can't handle the real world.

Clearly, there is no hope for the social justice warriors and the snowflakes, as both of them are factions of the Political Left, yet the reason why there is no hope for them is that they constantly complain about ridiculous and insane issues that are not really offensive. The only reason why the Political Left deems it offensive is that they do not like your lifestyle choices. It is apparent that these people on the Political Left need to take a look in the mirror in order to calm themselves down, but they will never do that because they want to change their views. It is certain for a fact that people of different cultures will always celebrate other cultures, including everything about different cultures. It is not offensive to celebrate different cultures and foreign holidays, as this constantly happens around the world. People who migrate to a new country are supposed to assimilate into their new culture and society in order to accept their new culture and heritage so that they can be successfully integrated into their new culture and society in their new country that they will call home, but not everyone will believe in this, as they have

---

[79] Ibid

no intention of integrating into the mainstream and or the rest of the society.

Nevertheless, the madness does not end there, as when a student saw a Trump sign at her university she started to scream, as the sign supported the agenda and promises made by Trump during the campaign as well as the law and the constitution.[80] Apparently, this student who screamed because she saw some Trump sign is stated to be an art major, and it can also be heard and seen on video that some people are trying to help her.[81] However, the only help that this student needs is that she demands that the police be called, and this is because she is probably triggered by seeing something associated with Donald Trump, as many other snowflakes and social justice warriors have a problem with obeying the law.[82] Clearly, this art student is a social justice warrior and a snowflake, because she refuses to see and hear the truth and the facts, as every time she sees the sign or for some other reason, she decides to scream and have a meltdown.[83] Yet, the liberal meltdowns from the social justice warriors and the snowflake factions of the known Political Left does not end there, as there is even more craziness at the college campuses around the United States of America. This time, the college craziness

---

[80] Rob Shimshock, "Watch This Student Scream At A Trump Sign For Two Minutes [VIDEO]," *Daily Caller*, May 12, 2017, http://dailycaller.com/2017/05/12/watch-this-student-scream-at-a-trump-sign-for-two-minutes-video/.

[81] Ibid

[82] Ibid

[83] Ibid

is from a student at Yale University who screams and shouts at a college professor.[84] The social justice warrior snowflake student at Yale does not believe a college or university of higher learning should be an intellectual environment.[85] No, instead, the social justice warrior snowflake student believes that a college and or university be a place that coddles and protects students from the dangerous world of what happens in the real world.[86] In other words, the social justice warrior snowflake student at Yale demands that college be a safe space that coddles and protects her and other students from the outside world of reality.[87]

Now, why was this social justice warrior snowflake student so angered, well it was because of an email sent by the professor's wife concerning Halloween costumes?[88] The reason why this social justice warrior snowflake student has a problem is because the professor's wife wrote an email to the students that told everyone that anyone should have the right to wear whatever they want for a Halloween costume.[89] Now, the social justice warrior snowflake student took offense to that email and believes that no one should wear anything

---

[84] Bre Payton, "Watch A Mob Of Yale Students Bully A Professor They Say Hurt Their Feelings," *The Federalist*, September 15, 2016, http://thefederalist.com/2016/09/15/watch-a-mob-of-yale-students-bully-a-professor-who-hurt-their-feelings/.

[85] Ibid

[86] Ibid

[87] Ibid

[88] Ibid

[89] Ibid

that is not about their cultural heritage. And, in fact, many other social justice warrior snowflake students have that same opinion, which of that wearing a costume on Halloween is culturally insensitive to that specific culture because you do not belong to that culture.[90] This provides further proof that the social justice warrior snowflake students have contempt for the constitution and the declaration of independence of the United States of America, as they do not want anyone to wear a costume from another culture if you are not part of that culture.[91]

Further, by not supporting the constitution and the declaration of independence of the United States of America, these social justice warrior snowflake students are infringing on other peoples' free speech rights, and they do not want to listen to the professor's wife as she is not in favor of limiting freedom and liberty concerning what people should and should not be allowed to wear.[92] But, the social justice warrior snowflake students do not care about that, as they believe people should be told of what they can and cannot wear; yet, at Yale, the minority students are the ones that have problems with Halloween costumes being worn by people.[93] And this claim from the minority students at Yale seems to make it similar to that of Black Lives Matter and other groups that hate the rule of law,

---

[90] Ibid

[91] Ibid

[92] Ibid

[93] Ibid

as it is clearly presented that they want to shut you down because they don't like what you are doing. Further, the professor tries to apologize but the social justice warrior snowflake students do not like it, and they also demand that the professor calls them by their given first name, even though the professor acknowledges that he has several hundred students.[94] Even more, the social justice warrior snowflake students think they can define their own meaning of what it means to be racist by citing their own personal experiences that they have had; well, if those social justice warrior snowflake students knew better, that is not how you define what racism and or racist means, but the social justice warrior snowflake students believes they can simply call the professor a racist because they do not like his response and the fact that anyone can wear anything they want to.[95] Clearly, these social justice warrior snowflake students are showing signs of irrational and psychotic anti-social behavior, as they do not want to follow the social standards and the norms of the United States of America, as well as the constitution and the declaration of independence. Additional irrational and psychotic anti-social behavior from the social justice warrior snowflake students at Yale is that they claim that the professor is the reason why a space for violence was created; and clearly, these students are delusional, as their behaviors are irrational, since they want to be protected and coddled in an environment that does not seek change or the truth,

---

[94] Ibid

[95] Ibid

but rather it is an isolated bubble.[96] And yet, another one of those social justice warrior snowflake student calls the professor a disgusting person with no regard for respect, as she does not like how he handled the situation.[97] But, whatever the professor said, they would not like it, as their behavior is irrational and delusional because they want to abolish the freedom of expression, the freedom of speech, and the freedom of the press. Nonetheless, another reason why these social justice warrior snowflake students is that of the term 'master' and 'associate master,' as they found it offensive, probably because the social justice warrior snowflake students want to equate those two terms to slavery, even though no proof exists.[98] It is nothing but political correctness, as the Political Left wants to silence people that they don't agree with.

Well, it seems we have a new form of madness going around the world, as now students and or other children are always being coddled and protected in a bubble with no criticisms exist. Yet, each time a social justice warrior makes a complaint, it shows that they are weak, as their reasoning is just another excuse for why they don't want to agree with conservatives and or Republicans. The fact of the matter is that these social justice warriors just care about themselves and no one care, even if they say they are promoters of Progress. You cannot help these social justice warriors, snowflakes, and or anyone of the Political Left, as they attempt to attack you for not adopting

---

[96] Ibid

[97] Ibid

[98] Ibid

their views, beliefs, opinions, and values. It is rather sad, as the Political Left wants to eliminate and or to abolish your freedom, liberty, free speech rights, as well as the entire constitution and the declaration of independence of the United States of America. The Political Left does not care what you say, as they only care and support what they agree with. The Political Left is the party of always obstructing stuff, and they believe it is their job to attack Trump because they don't like him. Clearly, this is just irrational and delusional behavior by the Political Left, but for some reason, the Political Left feels threatened by Trump, Pence, conservatives, and Republicans for no apparent reason. The Political Left feels threatened and or afraid of Trump, Pence, conservatives, and Republicans because they believe their rights are going to be infringed upon and or taken away, but there is no evidence of this; but, the Political Left are only afraid of Trump, Pence, conservatives, and Republicans because it is only in their head. As a result, if the Political Left wants to help out America and the rest of the world, it would be best if they learn and stop their irrational behavior and tactics.

To address reality, the Political Left and their factions need to stop with their hatred of people with different opinions, views, values, and beliefs. The Political Left needs to stop their political name calling, as calling someone a certain slur is not helping any society, as it is only dividing society. Nevertheless, the Political Left needs to be more open to accepting people. By all accounts, the Political Left needs to accept the constitution and the declaration of the United States of America, as well as freedom and liberty for everyone who live in the United States of America. And, in different countries around the world, the Political Left must accept freedom and liberty for all and that the government is not the solution, since government only infringes on peoples' right because they want to limit your freedom and liberty, along with your free speech rights. Provided that the Political Left listens to this book, they will understand why they must change their ways. In reality and or actuality, the role of government should be limited, as big government will attempt to control your freedom and liberty if it ever seeks to take more rights away from you.

Nevertheless, you do not want to be in a country such as Turkey that takes away your freedom and liberty, because they want to oppress and or suppress the opposition just because you not might agree with the government.

Chapter Three

Education, Jobs, and Taxation

Education and taxation is an interesting topic, as the

Political Left demands them as part of government spending, but the further reason is that the Political Left believes government should provide free college to all who is eligible and that taxes should be increased in order to finance the government. In other words, education is deemed as an entitlement whereas taxation is a tool to steal too much money from your hard-earned work, according to the Political Left.

Freedom, Liberty, and Government Overregulation

The goal of any type of higher education institution is to help facilitate knowledge in order to learn and obtain additional knowledge. Now, that was my basic definition of higher education, but that is not how the members of the Political Left see it, if they are a member of the social justice warrior and or snowflake faction. No, the social justice warrior and or snowflake factions see higher education as a safe space in order to save them from potential danger.[99] That is clearly delusional behavior, as when you go to college it is meant that you enhance your education or pursue some type of post-secondary education in order to pursue your dreams or to get a better job.

There is nothing but contempt from the Political Left, as they continue to demand free education to all, well to all who might qualify for free education. They think that everybody should be entitled to or needs to have a college degree. However, not everyone needs a college degree because it might not help the economy. Not everyone might benefit from a college degree, as sometimes it can useless in a way because of a slowed job market in which you have a college degree but you can't find a job anywhere. It is puzzling that a person originally got a college degree in order to start a career but then cannot get a job because no one will hire them. The excuse the employer(s) will say is that you might have a lack of experience in the field, even if a person is well-qualified. Well, there is a problem with

[99] Bre Payton, "Watch A Mob Of Yale Students Bully A Professor They Say Hurt Their Feelings," *The Federalist*, September 15, 2016, http://thefederalist.com/2016/09/15/watch-a-mob-of-yale-students-bully-a-professor-who-hurt-their-feelings/.

that excuse, which is how will a recent high school graduate get a job if they never have work experience. The further problem is that not all students in high school will have a job because they are too busy studying for exams and their classes in order to get passing grades just to be accepted into a good college and or university. Further, during college, not all students will seek or have a job, as they too are too busy with studying for their classes and any exams. It is not easy holding a job when you are a full-time high school or college student, as you have two responsibilities now: working and studying, the latter taking more time, depending on what your job is. Many high school students who have a job are limited to a certain amount of working hours because of labor laws put in place in order to prevent child abuse. College students, on the other hand, who do work, are usually only part-time students, if they are at a certain age, as they tend to have a family and need to pay the bills. On the other hand, college students who work might also be full time students, which are if they can handle the course load and work simultaneously, but not everyone can balance out their work life with their school life. So, that means each student who work and go to school at the same time will do so based upon their habits and scheduling. This means that the student will have to tell their employer of their course schedule so that the person responsible for making the schedule can make a more appropriate and desirable schedule that works around the classes of the students. What might seem easy is actually pretty complex; as not everyone might like the schedule and people will always complain. So, it will seem that anyone can complain because they are not getting a certain number of hours they want or they just hate how the entire schedule was made. This complaining about the schedule is fairly common, but some employers or people who make the schedule do it intentionally, as they might just be a jerk.

Considering that the schedule is an important piece of paper because it keeps track of the hours of each employee in their associated department, the schedule is a tool that tries to help people, but some people can make it better than others. The reasoning behind anything concerning scheduling can be a menial and labored task, but some people find pleasure in hurting people because they think they are better than everyone else. It is a case of notoriety because there seems to be something wrong with society. Yet, some people are just too pissed off or incompetent to make a decent schedule. It is something that the Political Left might use as the advantage to promote their businesses, but you actually thought most businesses were run by conservatives and or Republicans. Well, many of the large businesses are run by people who support and or donate to the Political Left. It makes practical sense for them to support and or donate to the Political Left because they want special deals associated with a government handout. Simply put, the businesses are meant to make a profit, but with many members of the Political Left owning or managing businesses, there can be a problem with how they function.

So, the focus is how to make a perfect schedule, well there is a problem there, as no schedule will be perfect, as it will be flawed if the person in charge of making the schedule gives all employees what they want. Well now, there is something to help you, as the scheduling is not the actual problem, because the actual problem is how to get a job if you never worked during high school and or at your time at college. It is certainly a challenge for many students to work during their high school years, as students would need to wake up before the time of dawn, but it depends on the city, the county, and the state you reside in. It is most important that you have experience according to the hiring managers, but what happens if you were too busy with school work and other studying. Well, if you seek out a job and are hired, it will be your lucky day, but your job search will take months and probably years. There is something about this that might make sense, but at the big businesses, the people in charge either support and or donate to the Political Left or they are part of the Political Left. It is certainly something that forces you to think about your future, but there is probably nothing that you can do about it.

For many reasons, people who apply to a job are many times considered to be underqualified, which simply means their education is lacking and or they have a lack of experience, yet they still think they are qualified for the job because it might advance their careers. At other times, people who apply to a job are overqualified, which is that they have too many post-secondary degrees and or their experience is equaled to that of a corporate executive. Then, there are the people who are perfectly qualified, as they either have the right level of education, experience, and or both. But, not all job candidates will be perfect, but it should not be a requirement that you have too much experience, as most of the time a basic high school diploma or a bachelor's degree is only required and or necessary. However, if you apply for a job that needs experience, it will usually consist of a licensing requirement in order to practice something, and this will usually require an internship as part of the education requirement. Now, this internship requirement will be part of the experience qualifications, even though it is mandated by the college and or university.

Yet, in the United States of America, you do not need a required internship to become a lawyer, but you do need to pass and graduate from law school as well as passing the bar. But, everything else that requires a license will require an internship as part of the education requirement to graduate, as this internship provides the student to gain firsthand experience of how they should function in their potential area of expertise. However, students now a days demand education as a place to party and ignore their worries. The Political Left has gotten worse over the years, and this time they demand free education because they believe it is best for the future, when really a person with a vocational degree will get paid much more than a person with a college degree, and that is because college graduates will probably get stuck with a minimum wage job that is not suitable of their qualifications. It is quite surprising that the job market is open, but some people are just lazy, as they do not want to work, but you need to start somewhere. Yet, many and or most recent college graduates believe they can get a job almost quickly right after they graduate, but that is just an illusion, unless you were really lucky with a hiring manager. But, certain fields might make you a better job candidate, such as if you majored in one of the STEM fields, which usually consist of science, technology, engineering, and or math, yet not all people might like those fields because they might find it too hard or they find it boring or uninteresting.

The major theme here is that college degrees are in demand but with the rise of college degrees, students will have more debt than ever, which will cost America too much money. It is a case of disinformation that the Political Left wants to use, as they claim it is part of the center of progress. Well, the meaning of Progress for the Political Left is to never look back, to ignore history, and to spend money that is not in existence. There might be a political force behind this, but you should remember that nothing can stop you from living your dreams of having the best career. Yet, if you constantly believe the Political Left about education, you will go into debt. You do not want to go into debt as a student, as student debt is not eligible for bankruptcy proceedings, but it you must use student debt for your education, make sure you get an internship or a paying job as fast as possible. Without a job or a paid internship, you will eventually go broke, unless you were one of those rich trust-fund babies.

It is essential that you learn, but it must be from a field that pays well; so this will mean you have to ignore the Political Left, because they will say everything is fine, but then you will be stuck with too much in student debt that will dry up your bank account(s). Remember, there is something that can help you, and that is called wisdom and the art of being confident, but not overconfidence, as overconfidence is a tactic that brainwashes you. The case-by-case basis of education is your goal to happiness. If you already have a job and you are happy, then you not might need a college degree, as you are happy with your high school diploma, your life, and your job. Just be confident, but it will actually help you in order to succeed. The goal of fascination is vital to your college education.

Again, if you are happy with your life because you believe you are where you want to be in life because of your high school diploma as well as your job, then you are fine, as you will probably have more and better opportunities for growth and promotions. In fact, your current job might be better for your life as a whole with just a high school diploma because college life could harm you. The way college will harm your life is that the professors might indoctrinate you with radical and extremist left-wing values, beliefs, and views. Now, some people who attend and or graduate from college are immune from that Political Left ideology, as they have faith in God and conservative and or Republican views and beliefs.

Nevertheless, you will find it difficult if you are a conservative and or Republican college student, as many of your friends can be very political because they don't believe in the actual constitution, as those friends of yours are actually part of the Political Left. When the Political Left attempts to use indoctrination on their own students in the college classrooms, it means that they do not respect your views, beliefs, and or values, as they want to replace them with a radical left-wing ideology. The piece of mind is to have faith and patience, as now-a-days it can be difficult in a college classroom. When this happens, you must make sure you do not lose any hope, but just be strong. No one can stop you from achieving your dreams, but you must remember that the Political Left is out to get you, as they want to make your education a political tool to rally against you. There is hope, but you must understand that the majority of college professors could be part of the Political Left, but some who are part of the Political Left do not want to become political in any manner, as they just want to teach. So, this means that they are not really part of the Political Left, but they still might be a Democrat when they vote. Yet, remember, education is part of life, and you will always have someone you know who hate a conservative and or a Republican ideology. Indoctrination is nothing new, as it currently occurs in the majority of college campuses, as they believe that their ideology is the best way for you to learn about stuff in school and to succeed in life.

Indoctrination is a way of life for certain people, as the goal is to brainwash you so you can be confused. However, this is not the type of indoctrination that involves pledging a sorority, fraternity, and or an honors society. No, this type of indoctrination is due to the Political Left faculty brainwashing you with their Radical Political Left ideologies. So, what happens here, well, they claim that their indoctrination efforts is because you need to integrate different cultures, views, opinions, values, and beliefs into your considerations and decisions. These Political Left college academics don't want you to think for yourselves, as they think that anything that promotes conservative and or Republican values is the definition of hatred, racism, misogyny, bigotry, sexism, Islamophobia, and other political name calling slurs. It is true that higher education is under attack, but money has nothing to do with it, since the United States Treasury can print as much money as they want; but the problem is that there is constant political correctness on the majority of college campuses, as it is a matter of extreme radical Political Left ideology that is caused by the support for liberalism.[100] For instance, one of the most common complaints by these Political Left social justice warrior snowflake students is the claim of white privilege,[101] but in fact, the term white privileged is being used as a racial slur against white people. The term white privilege is just a political attack by the Political Left social justice warrior snowflake students to slur and or to attack students who have a conservative and or Republican ideology. Another reason the Political Left social justice warrior snowflake students try to assert is that climate change is an important, and so if you don't agree with them then you must be denying science, which means those Political Left people will attack you in order to silence you for having a different ideology then them.[102] It is simply an attack by these Political Left social justice warrior snowflake students because they were brainwashed into

---

[100] Jeff Crouere, "Liberal Indoctrination Trumps Education at U.S. Colleges," *Town Hall*, December 10, 2016, https://townhall.com/columnists/jeffcrouere/2016/12/10/liberal-indoctrination-trumps-education-at-us-colleges-n2257882.

[101] Ibid

[102] Ibid

believing that climate change is bad for the earth, when really, the idea of climate change was only invented to promote bigger government, But, the Political Left does not care, and so they spew a fake narrative that climate change isn't normal and it will only harm society. In fact, climate change is not bad for society, and it is not as bad as the Political Left claims it to be, but it shall be discussed in the next chapter. Now, there is a case about why these Political Left social justice warrior snowflake students attack conservatives, Republicans, and people within their factions, as these Political Left social justice warrior snowflake students believe you should have the same ideology as them. Yet, these Political Left social justice warrior snowflake students only want to silence freedom of expression, freedom of speech, and freedom of the press, because they just don't want to agree with you. As a matter of fact, the Political Left social justice warrior snowflake students will never change their ways because they are so full of themselves. And with that, they keep on attacking.

The goal of Political Left college professors is to discourage and or to forbid students from having a conservative and or a Republican point of view, and this probably increased to an extreme level after Obama was elected, yet this Political Left ideology actually increased a lot after Donald Trump was elected as the President of the United States of America.[103] This Political Left ideology is nothing but bad for the rest of society. For instance, these Political Left social justice warrior snowflake students and their Political Left

---

[103] Ibid

professors team up to hold a rally in support of illegal immigration,[104] and that is because that the Political Left believes all illegal immigrants should be entitled to become automatic citizens, and it can be reflected that the Political Left just wants to use them to gain more support. Yes, it is true, the support of illegal immigration is part of the Political Left's ideological platforms, and it does not stop there, as some Political Left colleges through their Political Left professors and there Political Left social justice warrior snowflake students demand that their campus become a sanctuary for illegal immigrants.[105] Sure, it might sound good to those Political Left students and academics, but it is a violation of the law, as these people think that illegal immigrants who commit violent crimes should be always protected by providing them a safe space.[106] Well, it seems that these Political Left students and academics support the ideology of violence, as they even believe illegal immigrants who commit violent criminal acts should be rewarded for their behavior, but the Political Left institutions do not care about the federal laws,[107] even if they say it is part of their inclusion narrative. A safe space for violent criminal illegal immigrants is not only wrong, as it breaks federal laws on immigration,[108] but it also provides the reason why

---

[104] Ibid

[105] Ibid

[106] Ibid

[107] Ibid

[108] Ibid

there needs to be tougher laws regarding the harboring of illegal aliens and or criminal illegal alien fugitives.

Yet, these Political Left academics and students do not end there, as when a Somali refugee who was a student there committed a terrorist act, everyone was fearing for their life, which is the way I remember it from watching television; but, all of a sudden, there was now a black student group defending the terrorist known as the Coalition of Black Liberation,[109] which is probably part of the Black Lives Matter movement as well as being social justice warriors. The field of education people is such a mess that it isn't funny, because you have these radical and crazy domestic hate groups that promote Black Lives Matter, only because organizations such as the Coalition of Black Liberation believe too many black people are being violently killed by law enforcement.[110] There is a problem with this Political Left mentality, as these social justice warriors on college campuses actually believe they are being targeted daily, but they provide no evidence of this; yet these Black Nationalist movements actually believe a terrorist who harmed people is innocent.[111] This terrorist attack that occurred at Ohio State University is the reason why there must be strong immigration controls, but these Political Left academics and student will cry racism, bigotry, xenophobia, and Islamophobia, yet all they care about open borders. The Political Left

---

[109] Ibid

[110] Ibid

[111] Ibid

needs a reality check and they need to be better educated on the issues. What a bunch of craziness that is happening on college campuses, as this is why the Political Left students fail by simply complaining and whining over and over again. It is a sign that promotes a backwards ideology that only benefits Left-Wing radicalism, but the Political Left sees it as a necessary tactic to use on college campuses. This simply means that the Political Left wants to promote their contempt of freedom and liberty, as they want to block your voice if you have a different opinion. What a bunch of garbage the Political Left spews, as now these Political Left social justice warrior snowflake students demand they be called in the form or style of "Ze," as these college students believe that being called "He" or "She" is simply offensive, and that is just from snowflake transgendered students, which was sponsored by Tulane University student government association,[112] and that is not all. They only sponsored this specific pronoun legislation because Donald Trump won the 2016 Presidential election, and these Political Left students and academics believe that the result of the election has threatened them, but they never stated any evidence for their reasoning,[113] as their true intention for being threatened was due to them just being upset that Hillary Clinton lost, and so these college snowflake students decided to concoct a false narrative. Yet, really, it was all in their heads and or minds, as they have simply become too delusional. It is a mentality envisioned by the Political Left college professors in

---

[112] Ibid

[113] Ibid

order to promote the ideology that being politically correct is fine, that socialism and communism is the proper way to run your lives and government, and that there must be a vanguard to promote the idea of a radical Left-Wing ideology.

College indoctrination of students has become dangerous and needs to change, so it must be eliminated. Now, it has actually been admitted that the Political Left colleges and academics want to alter the ideology of students. You hear from television that these Leftist College professors are doing all kinds of crazy things, such as actually inciting riots and contributing as an accessory to a crime. There have been multiple reports on television that indicates Political Left protesters will riot outside of a college campus when a conservative and or Republican speaks at a sponsored event. Yet, in today's society, education is deemed as necessary, but not everyone needs a college degree. However, without a degree, you will be told that you will go nowhere in your life and that you will become a loner. Well, and then there is this idea that college should be free.

But, free college is a political talking point from the Political Left, especially from people such as Bernie Sanders, who basically believe free college should be a human right, as he says with every part of his platform. Now, free college might sound good, but it costs too much money, and that money needs to come from somewhere. So, where does it come from, well, it is financed by the state governments, but there is another problem here. When state governments spend money, they like to spend it on frivolous stuff, and this is especially true of the Political Left. So, when it comes to

101

free college, the Political Left will attempt to say it is free, but it is not free, as it needs to originate from somewhere. The Political Left will think it is fine to spend that money on free education, but the government will just go deeper into debt, as the Political Left in the government will say that it is necessary because it will provide a free service to poor people. Already, it was recently confirmed in April of 2017 that the state of New York declared free college for everyone, or so you think, but there is actually a catch you need to understand, or else you might face a consequence and or dilemma.[114] You see, in order to qualify for a free college education to a 2-year or 4-year college, your household will need to make less than or equal to $125,000.00, but that is not the consequence and or dilemma you will face if you want that free tuition.[115] The consequence that you will face is that you will need to pay all of that free money back to the state of New York or to some other entity, as there is a working and living requirement.[116] To put it into basic terms, you will have to pay back your scholarship (free money) back to the state of New York if you do not work and live in New York for the same time as it took you to complete the college degree program.[117] Simply put, if your degree program is 2-years in length, then you have to live and work in

---

[114] Anna Helhoski, "Why free college isn't always free," *Market Watch*, May 22, 2017, http://www.marketwatch.com/story/why-free-college-isnt-always-free-2017-05-22.

[115] Ibid

[116] Ibid

[117] Ibid

New York for a minimum of two years.[118] So, if you thought you would only stay in the state of New York for two years, you are wrong, as now you have to stay in the state for twice as long.[119] Two years become four years, while four years become eight years, or else your free money will turn into a government loan.[120] That is a pretty long time to spend in the state of New York just to get a free education, and you thought there were no special requirements. Well, this special requirement, as I will say, I do support, as it puts a check on government abuse and overuse, and by having this rule, the Political Left cannot abuse their powers in government. In other words, this rule attempts to prevent frivolous government spending. And then when those Political Left students find out about this rule, they will become upset and throw temper tantrums and commit violent criminal acts, because they want everything to be free, as paraphrased by a professor.[121] Sure, it is fine to have free college, as you won't have to pay it back, but some people don't like it because they say it will limit your freedom to work.[122] So, the argument of one supposedly Political Left academic believes it is wrong for someone to stay in the state of New York for the same length of the degree

[118] Ibid

[119] Ibid

[120] Ibid

[121] Ibid

[122] Carl Campanile, "Cuomo's free tuition program comes with a major catch," *New York Post*, April 11, 2017, http://nypost.com/2017/04/11/cuomos-free-tuition-program-comes-with-a-major-catch/.

program just because a college education was free.[123] But the thing about the free college education program in New York is that it requires students to enroll in public colleges and universities, which are either part of the City University of New York or the State University of New York, all of which consist of eighty-nine total higher education institutions.[124],[125] But, it is important that these students stay in the state of New York after completing their college degree in order to prevent entitlements from occurring.[126] But, yet again, the Political Left academic strikes again, as one states that some students might want to get a job in the state of California, and the reasoning behind that is that the Political Left wants to make free college as a entitlement program.[127] But, the Republicans were not having another entitlement program, as they knew it will cost too much money.[128]

Nevertheless, it will continue to amaze people of why college should not be free. But, they are the Political Left, so they think that everything should be free. Well, free college is not free, as it actually

---

[123] Ibid

[124] Anna Helhoski, "Why free college isn't always free," *Market Watch*, May 22, 2017, http://www.marketwatch.com/story/why-free-college-isnt-always-free-2017-05-22.

[125] Carl Campanile, "Cuomo's free tuition program comes with a major catch," *New York Post*, April 11, 2017, http://nypost.com/2017/04/11/cuomos-free-tuition-program-comes-with-a-major-catch/.

[126] Ibid

[127] Ibid

[128] Ibid

costs money, and that money comes from government tax payers who have jobs and pay into the system, if they are required to. So, what else sounds interesting was Bernie Sanders proposed free college program, and this would basically consist of making all public universities and public colleges tuition-free, but essentially the plan calls for the entire United States Government to pay for the tuition.[129] Basically, Bernie Sanders believes it is important to make public colleges and public universities free to anyone who qualifies is because of Germany, Chile, Norway, Finland, Sweden, and several other countries, but he fails to mention that those are much smaller countries with smaller amounts of national debt.[130] At the same time, Bernie Sanders wanted the federal government of the United States of America to cover the free cost of tuition for every eligible person who attends a public college and or a public university.[131] However, this is an extremely bad and dangerous idea for the federal government to take on, as the national debt is too high as it currently stands, probably the highest it is ever been in the history of the United States of America. Yet, when you tell to someone of the Political Left that college is a privilege and not a right, they will probably claim you are undermining and disenfranchising us from pursuing our dreams. Well, clearly, those on the Political Left who say their dreams are being undermined and disenfranchised do not

---

[129] Friends of Bernie Sanders, It's Time to Make College Tuition Free and Debt Free, https://berniesanders.com/issues/its-time-to-make-college-tuition-free-and-debt-free/.

[130] Ibid

[131] Ibid

actually understand the real world, as everything in the real world costs money, so someone has to pay for it.

No one is denying anyone to a college education, but the Political Left does not understand that, as they believe they should receive it as an entitlement that they do not have to pay for. They (the Political Left) have no clue about the reality that they live in, as they still think everything is free, yet they are just arrogant and ignorant. It is actually a sad case of not understanding the consequences, since everything does cost money to spend. But, as a matter of fact, college used to be free or at a reduced in some states, but that was back until the 1980s, and this was probably due to the United States not being in a lousy debt situation.[132] So, what is the best part of this plan by Bernie Sanders, well the only thing that is good about it was that it would limit new interest rates of new loans around 2.37 percent.[133] Yet, the interest rates of current student loans were only to be decreased to the current lowest interest rates.[134] So, how do people pay for all of this, well Bernie Sanders wants to implement a new tax on Wall Street speculation, and his reasoning for this is because he blames Wall Street for a financial collapse in 2007 and it is done in other countries.[135] But wait, there's more, as Bernie Sanders wants you to work to gain valuable career experience,

---

[132] Ibid

[133] Ibid

[134] Ibid

[135] Ibid

and most likely, the Political Left will probably refuse to work because it is only the federal minimum wage.[136] In addition, Bernie Sanders would just increase spending without reducing the national debt,[137] as that is the Political Left likes to do. Nevertheless, there are some people who demand free tuition at college just because they are black, or as some people refer to as African-American,[138] even though the term African-American is only used in the United States of America, as every other country labels black people as where they are from. For example, if you were a black person from South Africa you will be called a black South African. To get back to the point, the Black Lives Matter movement is the cause of black people wanting free college just for their own race/ethnicity, as they believe they are so special and are entitled to reparations just because they are black.[139] Well, what we have here is that self-described Political Left social justice warrior students who happen to be black want their college education to be free of charge because of slavery.[140] Even more, these Political Left social justice warrior students who happen to be black and probably part of the Black Lives Matter movement

---

[136] Ibid

[137] Ibid

[138] Jon Street, "University's student government wants free tuition 'reparations' for black students," *The Blaze*, April 19, 2017, http://www.theblaze.com/news/2017/04/19/universitys-student-government-wants-free-tuition-reparations-for-black-students/.

[139] Ibid

[140] Ibid

believe they are entitled to receive reparations due to slavery that occurred long, long ago, even though they have never actually been subjected to slavery.[141] These Political Left social justice warrior students demand that only black people have their college tuition be free of charge because they find it hard to apply to colleges when they fill out the application as well as because of complaining about not enough black people being accepted.[142]

Well, here is a problem with that Political Left argument, as colleges and universities have a standard to accept a pre-defined amount of students, as space is limited, and not every person of color can get accepted. But, if you tell this to a Black Lives Matter member or to some social justice warrior, then they will attack you and call you racist for simply stating a fact that not everyone meets the requirements. To them, it is simply a delusional problem, as the Black Lives Matter movement and the social justice warriors want everything for free, including their education. But, then they also cry the diversity and inclusion complaint, but their problem has nothing to do with diversity or inclusion, as they believe everything should be free to them because they want it to be free of charge.[143] But here is what actually happened at that Kentucky University: it got voted down by the college administration because the administrators who oversee the college and are part of the board of trustees do not see it

---

[141] Ibid

[142] Ibid

[143] Ibid

as a reality as they view it as a ridiculous and insane demand.[144] In fact, the exact reasoning that college administrators gave for rejecting the resolution was that it does not represent an official position of what the college believes in.[145] In other words, the college does not really recognize that demand because it is an illegitimate issue, since it is an insane resolution.[146]

Nevertheless, this same tactic by social justice warriors to make college tuition for black students was also utilized at the University of Wisconsin in Madison, and this time they demanded free housing in addition to free tuition as well as a similar type of task-force for any black student.[147] Now, what was demanded in Wisconsin would cost about twenty thousand dollars per black college student, and this would probably continue until the student graduates.[148] And again, the argument that was made was about diversity and inclusion, yet as stated before, diversity and inclusion to the Political Left only means that you do not apply if you are a conservative and or a Republican.[149] So, basically, you are

---

[144] Julia Glum, "No free tuition for black students despite slavery reparations resolution at western Kentucky," *News Week*, April 21, 2017, http://www.newsweek.com/western-kentucky-free-tuition-black-students-587677.

[145] Ibid

[146] Ibid

[147] Ibid

[148] Ibid

[149] Ibid

automatically excluded because you have a different perspective or point of view, as the Political Left wants everyone to be the same as them as well as being politically correct. But at the same time, the social justice warriors at Wisconsin blame ACT and SAT scores that were black students took during high school years is part of the overall problem.[150] However, the most insane that these social justice warriors stated was that using ACT and SAT scores in the application and acceptance process promotes and or upholds white supremacy because opportunities are restricted for the poor people, which is simply hogwash.[151] Well, here is the problem with that type and manner of argument given by those social justice warriors who only want black people to have free tuition and or free housing[152]: it openly promotes racism because only one race/ethnicity should have the access to a free college education, it has been demonstrated that poor and or homeless people can gain access to an institution of higher education, and that college admission scores might not reflect how well a potential student will succeed in college. According to some students at the school in Wisconsin, some students do not agree that it was fair, saying that it was also odd just to offer an entitlement to just black student, while another student says the

---

[150] Associated Press, "Wisconsin students demand free college for African-Americans," *Associated Press*, February 17, 2017, http://nypost.com/2017/02/17/wisconsin-students-demand-free-college-for-african-americans/.

[151] Ibid

[152] Ibid

amount of scholarships should be increased.[153] From the consensus of specific students, they do not believe in free handouts and that you need to earn that education by working hard.[154] Well, when those social justice warrior snowflake students hear these statements from their other student peers, they will start calling those students who oppose the free handout political name slurs. It is truly sad that this is the way that the Political Left wants to get their message out, but they are delusional and many of them still live in their parents' basement refusing to work because they want everything to be a free handout. And yet, the Political Left still supports higher taxes even if it hurts them and their family, but they probably won't care until they see the invoice.

In retrospect, there is also the issue of taxes, which is somehow tied to jobs and education, but for the rest of this chapter, we shall only discuss jobs and taxes. In the meantime, politicians generally disagree with each other on tax policy in the Republican Party, but they agree that taxes should not overburden people and businesses. On the other hand, Democrats and the members of the Political Left believe that all taxes should increase on the millionaires and billionaires, such as that of Senator Bernie Sanders. People who identify as being a member of the Political Left believe everyone should pay their fair share of taxes but so do conservatives and Republicans. Yet, for the Political Left, they demand that millionaires and billionaires should pay higher tax rates based upon their income

---

[153] Ibid

[154] Ibid

levels. So, what you have here is that the people of the Political Left demand that millionaires and billionaires should pay the majority of the taxes in the United States of America. But what the Political Left fails to understand is that the millionaires and the billionaires pay almost every tax payer's fair share of income taxes to the federal government.[155] What's even more embarrassing for the Political Left's argument is that a little over forty-five percent of Americans do not actually pay any type of income tax at all, and many people in that forty-five percent bracket actually pay something that is known as a negative income tax.[156] The reason that so many Americans do not pay an income tax is because they do not make enough money; and for the people who have a negative income tax they are eligible for tax breaks, which means their entire tax liability for paying an income taxes to the federal government is actually erased from existence.[157] Further, the Political Left is wrong about increasing the income tax rates because already sixty-nine percent of millionaires and billionaires already pay the majority of all federal taxes while eighty-seven percent of all the rich people pay federal income taxes.[158]

---

[155] Mark J. Perry, "CBO study shows that 'the rich' don't just pay a 'fair share' of federal taxes, they pay almost everybody's share," *AEI*, June 13, 2016, https://www.aei.org/publication/cbo-study-shows-that-the-rich-dont-just-pay-a-fair-share-of-federal-taxes-they-pay-almost-everybodys-share"/.

[156] Catey Hill, "45% of Americans pay no federal income tax," *Market Watch*, April 18, 2016, http://www.marketwatch.com/story/45-of-americans-pay-no-federal-income-tax-2016-02-24.

[157] Ibid

[158] Ibid

So, it seems that the argument made by the Political Left has been proven wrong; and currently, the United States of America is one of the highest taxed countries in the world. But, instead of increasing federal taxes, they should be reduced, as it does actually promote growth. Yet, the Political Left still believes in higher taxes because they think it will provide more revenue to the federal government, but it actually forces businesses to move to countries like Canada and Ireland. In reality, the Political Left is delusional, as the rich people already pay enough in taxes, yet they still want higher tax rates because of a spending problem and something known as redistribution of wealth. What is redistribution of wealth you say, well it simply means taking back money from the rich and giving it to the poor, something you already might heard of because it is a modern day Robin Hood but only a government entity.

Well, here is the problem with redistribution of wealth: it takes money from the richest and then gives it to the poorest in the form of welfare to pay for benefits through taxation.[159] So, the Political Left believe the poorest people deserve some type of welfare, well, if you work for it then it is fine. However, the Political Left does not want to put in any type of work requirement, as they want to give everything away for free. Many people who classify as being poor or part of the working class do not like the idea that the government giving away welfare benefits to the people who did not earn them, yet the Political Left fails to understand this. The people

---

[159] Business Dictionary, Redistribution of Wealth, http://www.businessdictionary.com/definition/redistribution-of-wealth.html.

who worked hard for their money finds it disheartening that people are getting a free ride off of their income that was paid to the federal government. When people get welfare, it creates a dependence on government because the welfare benefits are being acknowledged as an automatic entitlement that will always be paid; thus, people will not work because they are depending on the government to always pay them.[160] Yet, it does not end there, as the Political Left still demands higher taxes, as they also believe in the death tax or what is known by an inheritance tax. Now, the death tax is simply a tax on the decedent's heirs of the estate. This means once the decedent dies then the heirs to his/her estate will be liable to pay the taxes on that estate.

First of all, the heirs to the decedent's estate never actually earned that money, as it was an inheritance to them when the decedent died. Now, what the death tax basically does is that it makes the heirs of the estate to become liable for the tax bill. This actually burdens the heirs to pay a penalty to the federal government, just because their decedent passes away, but the Political Left does not see it that way. No, the Political Left believes it is necessary because it generates income for the government, and as you know the Political Left wants to spend money that they don't have. It is just another way for the Political Left to spend your money to provide for welfare benefits or their art of what you know as redistribution of wealth. In

---

[160] Daniel Mitchell, "Redistribution of Wealth Does Not Stimulate Economic Growth," *CNS News*, May 24, 2016, http://www.cnsnews.com/commentary/daniel-mitchell/redistribution-wealth-does-not-stimulate-economic-growth.

other words, redistribution of wealth is basically some legal form of a partial pyramid or Ponzi scheme, but the only reason it is legal is because it is mandated by the federal government of the United States of America. Yet, the Political Left still sees the death tax as a necessary incentive because it can help the poor, but in actuality it will only give people a free handout, and many of those people who get those free handouts in the form of welfare benefits do not work, as they believe they don't need to work because they are getting a free ride from the government. Essentially, the Political Left does not care, as they believe government should tell you how much tax you should pay.

Nevertheless, when all else fails, create another law that purports to create jobs, but it is actually a tax bill in disguise. The Political Left has done this time and time again, but they think it is necessary because they just want more money for the government. The Political Left fails to understand that their jobs bill will actually create things worse for the populace of the United States of America, as unpatriotic government bureaucrats will attempt to game the system by fining everyone they can in order to abuse the tax system. It is essentially legal theft because the government mandates it, yet these laws are actually bad for the economy and the entire working class. The Political Left says it promotes their ideology of being progressive, but to them progressive means to go backwards by using the outdated systems of Socialism, Communism, and or Marxism. Yet, they don't see it that way, as the majority of the Political Left sees capitalism as the enemy of the state, but when they actually have a business then they decide to engage in this idea of capitalism, so they are hypocrites. Yet, the Political Left sees taxes as a necessary tool to enforce the rule of law, but certain members of the Political Left had problems paying taxes, such as Timothy Geithner and Al Sharpton. However, Al Sharpton and Timothy Geithner were never arrested for tax crimes, and even more, it is possible that Al Sharpton did not get arrested because Obama did not see Al Sharpton as a problem for society. In the meantime, the type of tax policy that is instituted will depend on what people want, but it should follow the constitution and the rule of law as well as being fair. On the other hand, the tax plans must be evaluated and reconsidered, as when the Political Left writes them then it can become really bad. Neither side might win, but it must be a fair plan.

Simply put the problems with certain tax plans and tax laws are that they seem to be intrusive and possibly an abuse of power by giving certain agencies too much power. By this, we mean the government will abuse the power, because it essentially gives the appropriate government agencies an unlimited amount of power. For instance, FATCA and FBAR were an abuse of government power, were the latter (FBAR) is described as protecting bank secrecy but it actually does not do that at all.[161] On the other hand, FATCA is something different but similar, but I say it is just an abuse of power. However, FBAR or what is known as the bank secrecy act is actually a law that targets money laundering, so it seems that the United

---

[161] Internal Revenue Service, "Bank Secrecy Act," September 27, 2016, https://www.irs.gov/businesses/small-businesses-self-employed/bank-secrecy-act.

States Government did not care about banking secrecy like Switzerland did.[162] In fact, the bank secrecy act is actually a law that attempts to police money laundering crimes of any nature, and in turn, criminals will be held accountable.[163] Yet, when you look at this bank secrecy act closely, you will see the name as a misnomer, as it has nothing to do with protecting banking secrecy for a person or a business entity. Instead, the bank secrecy act requires business transactions ten thousand dollars and above to be reported to the federal government and the reason for this argument is to prevent money laundering and or other types of financial crimes.[164] Well, isn't that interesting, as the federal government automatically thinks you and your business are conducting some sort of criminal enterprise if you don't report your business transactions of ten thousand dollars and above. And, what happens if you try to divide that business transaction of ten thousand dollars and above into multiple deposits into your bank account, well the government will accuse you of a crime of what is known as structuring. You see, the government thinks it is entitled to know your daily routine and how your business operates from day-to-day. In fact, the federal government can only collect taxes if your business meets the specific requirements of owing taxes. In reality, the federal government has overstepped their boundaries and has abused their powers given to them that were

---

[162] Ibid

[163] Ibid

[164] Ibid

granted by the constitution. Now, if you think the bank secrecy act was passed by Republicans in Congress, well you are wrong, as it was actually passed by Democrats by a large majority, because both houses at the time of passing had a Democratic majority: fifty-seven Democratic Senators and two-hundred and forty-three Democratic members of the House of Representatives.[165] So, now you know why the bank secrecy actually passed: because the Political Left had the majority of seats in both chambers of Congress.[166] And if that wasn't enough, Richard Nixon was the President at the time, yet Nixon just signed it into law, and the possible reason was because is that Nixon wanted to be tough on crime. And yet, when you look at the final vote in the House of Representatives, you will see that 161 Democrats voted to pass and so did 141 Republicans, but you will also see that eighty-two Democrats did not vote to pass along with forty-four Republicans joining those eighty-two Democrats.[167] In actuality, 302 politicians voted to pass the bill, while the others abstained.[168] If such a bank secrecy act was proposed today, it will most likely fail, because the Republicans are more conservative than ever before and they are skeptical of big brother, also known as big government. In fact, today, most conservatives and or the majority of

---

[165] Wikipedia, 91st United States Congress, https://en.wikipedia.org/wiki/91st_United_States_Congress.

[166] Ibid

[167] GovTrack, To pass H.R. 15073, A bill to amend the Federal Deposit Insurance Act to require insured banks to maintain certain records, to require that certain transactions in U.S. currency be reported to the Department of the Treasury, https://www.govtrack.us/congress/votes/91-1970/h255.

[168] Ibid

Republicans want less government in their lives, as they do not want the government to tell them what they can and cannot do, but the Political Left supports big government and does not actually care about the little people they claim to support. Yet, we need to remember that the Political Left wants to take away your freedom, liberty, and rights, while also protesting simultaneously that they are being attacked. What a bunch of hypocrites the Political Left is, and it just shows you that they do not understand reality. What they do know is that they want to control your lives with more government, and yet people still support them.

We need to understand that the FBAR must be repealed because it is a frivolous and over-reaching law, as it always automatically assumes that business transactions of ten-thousand dollars and above are part of a criminal act.[169] It seems that some things will never change, as the Political Left promotes government theft with their high taxes and tax rates, and it seems that they believe it is justifiable because it will provide for a redistribution of wealth from the rich to the poor in order to provide for welfare benefits to people who don't deserve them because they refuse to work. Yet, at a closer look, you will see that this FBAR or bank secrecy act is an abuse of government power, as it also demands people who live and work overseas to report their foreign bank account assets if it reaches a certain amount, and again, the reasoning behind this is to prevent

---

[169] Internal Revenue Service, "Bank Secrecy Act," September 27, 2016, https://www.irs.gov/businesses/small-businesses-self-employed/bank-secrecy-act.

financial crimes.[170] Well, here is what that actually means for US expats living overseas to report their foreign assets of their foreign bank account(s) if it reaches a certain amount of money[171]: the federal government automatically thinks every single US expat who live and work overseas are guilty of not paying their taxes to the Internal Revenue Service. In order words, you are considered an automatic tax cheat just for living and working abroad. Yet, the Political Left still thinks that this is necessary in order to give the government more money, but they are just out of touch with reality. In reality, the bank secrecy act needs to go away, and if you don't report your foreign assets you could be charged with a crime, yet the Political Left do not actually care.

Similarly, FATCA is just as bad and even worse than the bank secrecy act, but this time it was a law passed by a Political Left majority in both chambers of Congress with a Political Left President named Barrack Hussain Obama. The Foreign Account Tax Compliance Act is part of the larger HIRE Act, but the former shall only be discussed, yet FATCA demands the same thing as FBAR, in which there is some sort of reporting requirements for banks.[172] Basically, FATCA forces foreign financial institutions and foreign non-financial institutions to report their U.S. customers' financial

---

[170] Ibid

[171] Ibid

[172] Internal Revenue Service, "Foreign Account Tax Compliance Act," September 13, 2016, https://www.irs.gov/businesses/corporations/foreign-account-tax-compliance-act-fatca.

foreign assets.[173] At the same time, FATCA also mandates that US tax payers report any foreign financial assets if a certain requirement is met.[174] However, if a US tax payer holds any assets that are in an offshore (outside the jurisdiction of the United States of America) financial institution, they might still be required to report that information, and if they do not report it then a penalty could be assessed.[175] Now, this reporting requirement is said to be a minimum of at least fifty-thousand dollars, and when reporting these foreign assets an additional form will be filed with the income tax owed to the United States federal government.[176]

If you think this FATCA and FBAR reporting requirement is insane and ridiculous, then you are exactly correct, as the only reason why this exists is because of big government supporters and people who don't know how the economy works. Now, get this, even though you are a US expat who lives and works in a foreign country outside of the United States of America, you still owe the federal government some form of money, because the United States of America is one of two countries that only taxes on worldwide income, the other of which is Eritrea. However, I am a firm believer that US expats who live and work abroad should not pay any income

---

[173] Ibid

[174] Internal Revenue Service, "Summary of FATCA Reporting for U.S. Taxpayers," November 7, 2016, https://www.irs.gov/businesses/corporations/summary-of-fatca-reporting-for-u-s-taxpayers.

[175] Ibid

[176] Ibid

taxes to the United States federal government, because they still have to pay potential income taxes to the country in which they live and work. Yet, the Political Left still believes all US expats should pay income tax, only because they believe it will help fund the federal government. Yet, the rest of the world, excluding Eritrea, does not tax on worldwide income, and by both of these two countries doing this tactic, it amounts to double taxation, and double taxation is not right, but it goes against the founding principles of the United States of America.

So, how does the United States federal government enforce this reporting requirement, well they (the Political Left) decided to draft and then implement intergovernmental agreements (IGAs) with the other governments of the world.[177] Now, if you think these IGAs are actually constitutional and legal, you are actually mistaken, because these IGAs are actually individual treaties between the United States of America and individual foreign governments.[178] However, the Political Left does not care, because they do not like the constitution, and they will attempt to avoid Senate ratification as much as possible and even former Secretary of State John Kerry said something similar to that. The Political Left has wants to destroy the constitution because they want to abuse their power by giving more power to the government. Essentially, the Political Left does not

---

[177] U.S. Department of the Treasury, Foreign Account Tax Compliance Act (FATCA), March 29, 2017, https://www.treasury.gov/resource-center/tax-policy/treaties/Pages/FATCA.aspx.

[178] Ibid

really believe in Senate Ratification, as they only support the United Nations and other globalist organizations that promote the ideology of big government will always be better for anyone.

Now, the Political Left states FATCA was passed to combat tax evasion, but it actually does not stop it because it hurts everyone else. It only exists to exert an abuse of government authority. There is actual evidence that FATCA hurts the people, as it targets the financial privacy of too many people, as well as penalizing foreign financial institutions because they carry the costs of actually reporting such information to the federal government.[179] It can actually cost too much for compliance, such as between two-hundred billion dollars and one trillion dollars, yet the Political Left does not care about the costs, all they care about is spending.[180] And, the Political Left still claimed that between one-hundred and one-hundred and fifty billion dollars were lost to the idea of tax evasion, yet each study conducted refuted that claim.[181] In other words, that idea that between 100 and 150 billion dollars of taxes is lost due to tax evasion is simply over exaggerated.[182] At the same time, you will hear news reports and first-hand accounts that US expats have to give up their citizenship because of the insane reporting requirements of FATCA,

---

[179] Veronique De Rugy, "Is It Time to Repeal FATCA?," *Town Hall*, April 27, 2017, https://townhall.com/columnists/veroniquederugy/2017/04/27/is-it-time-to-repeal-fatca-n2318631.

[180] Ibid

[181] Ibid

[182] Ibid

FBAR, and the fact that foreign banks are refusing to open bank accounts of US expats who live and work in foreign countries.[183] Yet, when you tell this information to the Political Left, they just keep on saying that there is no correlation between giving of citizenship with that of FATCA, well they are certainly mistaken, because they still believe every US expat is a tax cheat. The reason why it is hurting US expats is because of banking regulations, and since US expats cannot open a bank account in a foreign country, it hurts their financial standings; and there is a direct correlation between US expats giving up their US citizenship with that of the FATCA law.[184] Yet, even if you explain that to the Political Left, they still say otherwise, as they are actually in La La Land. The Political Left are in their own little reality because they are out of touch with the working class. Nevertheless, some Republican members of Congress have made it clear that they will attempt to repeal this terrible, bad, dangerous, and unconstitutional law, as well as the unconstitutional IGAs.[185] At the same time, repealing this terrible, bad, dangerous, and unconstitutional law known as FATCA was a major part of the 2016 Republican National Convention platform;[186] yet the Political Left does not like this idea of repealing FATCA, reducing corporate tax

---

[183] Ibid

[184] Ibid

[185] Ibid

[186] Republican Overseas, GOP includes anti-FATCA and pro-RBT language in their 2016 Platform, https://republicansoverseas.com/timeline/gop-includes-anti-fatca-language-2016-platform/.

rates, and abolishing the citizenship-based tax system with a territorial system, as it does not fit the ideology of the Political Left.[187] The Political Left is just out of touch, and they still believe a jobs bill is required just to provide jobs to the populace. Well, there is a problem with that reasoning, as government does not create private sector jobs for people. The Political Left believes that the federal government can create private sector jobs because of spending and or investing, yet by doing that you get nothing but government waste, so it is just a waste of money.[188] Now, the federal government can create government jobs such as joining the military or becoming part of the large federal bureaucracy by becoming a government employee, which is seen as direct employment.[189] Now, the federal government can simply be an indirect employer, yet that is not what it seems to be, because you are not actually working for the government, and in the end, this only works well with the construction companies as employment simply just increases.[190] Nevertheless, the Political Left will say that that statement is confirmation that government creates jobs but it is not, as those jobs in the construction industry might only be temporary, and it is actually up to the businesses to hire people. You see, the government does not create those private-sector

---

[187] Citizens for Tax Justice Staff, "The Five Worst Tax Policy Proposals in the 2016 Republican Party Platform," *Tax Justice Blog*, July 20, 2016, http://www.taxjusticeblog.org/archive/2016/07/the_five_worst_tax_policy_prop.php#.WStqn4zyvIU.

[188] Mark Ahlseen, "Why Government Can't Create Jobs," *FEE*, October 01, 1993, https://fee.org/articles/why-government-cant-create-jobs/.

[189] Ibid

[190] Ibid

construction jobs or any other types of jobs, as it is up to the owners of that business or the employer itself if it is large enough, to offer jobs to people. If the employer wants to build some type of infrastructure as part of a government contract and or program, then that employer will decide to hire any necessary people, but if the government approves them as a contractor, that money will mainly go to materials and supplies since that is what is needed to build the infrastructure. Instead, the employer will pay the employees out of their own pocket from fees, which does consist of any money left over from that original proposed budget for materials and supplies. When the Political Left says government will create jobs, it just adds to the deficit and the national debt, as it is just a spending program. Government does not create private sector jobs, because it is the responsibility of the business owner and or employer to offer jobs and then to offer inventory to sell to consumers or to simply provide a service that offers a service to consumers and to other businesses. It is especially funny when President Obama stated that business owners did not create their own business from the ground up,[191] but it is also offensive, because those people who started those businesses devoted their personal finances and own time to build that business from the ground up. When Obama stated that, he thinks that the government actually built and started the business you started and built from the ground up, or as he said, "you didn't build

---

[191] John Stossel, "Government Doesn't Create Jobs," *Reason*, April 29, 2015, http://reason.com/archives/2015/04/29/how-are-jobs-created.

that."[192] You see, the Political Left such as FDR, Obama, communists, and socialists do not support the idea of free market capitalism, but the free market is regulated, yet the Political Left wants to overregulate it in order be in complete control of it.[193] Now, when the Political Left demands higher wages, the employers, if they are large enough and or have enough money, then they will fully or partially automate the entire assembly line, such as what McDonalds did when they replaced cashiers with automated kiosks,[194] and many other fast food restaurants have decided to go this route because of the demand of a higher minimum wage. Yet, Nancy Pelosi and many others who make up the Political Left still believe you need to have a jobs bill to create jobs in general,[195] but what she doesn't realize is that it is up to the free market economy and the business owners to create jobs, as there is this thing known as supply and demand.

Nevertheless, the Political Left just does not get it, as they are actually completely clueless on education, jobs, and taxation; yet the Political Left wants more government and still wants to shut you down because they don't respect the rights of others: this includes white people, conservatives, libertarians, and Republicans. The Political Left is just out of touch and just wants to spend your money

---

[192] Ibid

[193] Ibid

[194] Ibid

[195] Susan Jones, "Pelosi: Trump 'Has No Jobs Bill'; 'They've Done Nothing'," *CNS News*, February 27, 2017, http://www.cnsnews.com/news/article/susan-jones/pelosi-trump-has-no-jobs-bill-theyve-done-nothing.

to waste on more government spending programs that actually hurts the economy. It is a part of life, but more government does not actually mean a better and more vibrant economy. The free market economy must survive because it shall supply and demand any and all jobs that are needed and or are required in a society.

Yet, an increase in taxes will only hurt people, as it simply takes out more money out of your paycheck. On the other hand, the Political Left needs to be more tolerant and accepting on college campuses and everywhere else, as the Political Left wants to obstruct people who have differing perspectives than them. So, it would seem there is work to do, but it is possible. In order to have better education reform, it must be conservative and not offer too many entitlements or free handouts. In order to have better and or more jobs, we must rely upon the free market, as supply and demand should be in force, and it should not be mandated by government. In order to provide better taxes, the government must keep special interests and other lobbyists out of the reform, and we must make sure it is fair.

However, taxes should be competitive with that of other countries, such as Ireland, as lower taxes provide better supply and demand. Nevertheless, we must make sure that the Political Left does not get what they want, as their plans and visions for the future can hurt everything, which in the end will be a disaster.

Chapter Four

Immigration and Science

The role of immigration and science has been constantly

debated everywhere, but the Political Left just does not care, as they want open borders and believe that coal is ruining everything. The Political Left is just clueless. The very meaning of Democracy for the Political Left now-a-days is that of supporting illegal immigration and an open borders society. It is the reason that the Political Left is out of touch with reality, but they seem to think that illegal immigration and or illegal immigrants is a good thing, as they believe it helps the economy and improves and increases the workforce. Well, for starters, illegal immigration does increase the workforce, but it actually diminishes it at the same time because it takes away jobs from qualified legal residents and citizens of the United States of America. Yet, the Political Left still refuses to accept that illegal immigration is bad for the United States of America.

Instead, the Political Left demands that every single illegal immigrant be given US citizenship, and the reason why they want to give automatic US citizenship to illegal immigrants is because the Political Left supports open borders. Illegal immigration is actually a crime in the United States of America, just like it is in other countries, but for some reason the Political Left wants to ignore that part of federal law. No one can actually explain why the Political Left wants to support the idea of illegal immigration as each person has a different theory; yet, one of the most probable and one of the most relevant theories is that the Political Left wants to give the immigrants automatic citizenship because they left their country out of fear, and that is most likely true. However, if this is the reason the Political Left supports illegal immigration, and then it would only mean one thing: that the Political Left is using them to gain more and more popularity with their voting base. It is essentially some type of faux issue that the Political Left cares about, as they are only using these illegal immigrants. The reason the Political Left are using these illegal immigrants is due to the fact that they want the votes of those illegal immigrants. Then, after the Political Left gets the vote from those illegal immigrants, the Political Left decides to not care about those illegal immigrants anymore. It is a proven tactic engineered by someone who wants to create a false flag, that the Political Left will provide a utopian society to anyone who wants to escape violence, criminality, oppression, and suppression. However, the Political Left is just using that false flag of a utopian society to illegal immigrants as a ploy to get votes.

The reason why the Political Left demands illegal immigrants be given citizenship is because they say they are hard-working and that they escaped a very dangerous country because of a hostile situation, which would then make those illegal immigrants refugees. Well, that is not how a person actually gets legal asylum or becomes an actual refugee. No, in order to become an actual refugee and to seek legal asylum according to the laws of every and or most nations, one must usually enter an embassy or even a consulate of a foreign country and provide an actual written statement of why and if they are seeking asylum. The person who seeks asylum as a legal refugee could also just provide a written statement of seeking asylum. But the Political Left does not see illegal immigration that way, as the Political Left wants to make up their own laws. You see, in the United States, all asylum and or refugees must be vetted and complete the appropriate paperwork before being allowed to migrate to the United States of America, but in other countries this is not the case, as in Europe, the European Union initiated some sort of quota system, and the person is vetted and processed after they arrive in the new country. Yet, if you are opposed to mass-migration, you are called political name slurs. Nevertheless, all of this shall be discussed later in the chapter.

For one thing, illegal immigrants getting citizenship is really wrong and should be illegal, as it is illegal, but the Political Left does not care about traditions, as they want to change and ignore the past. It is pretty clear that the Political Left hates the United States of America and her traditions, no matter how reprehensible they are, but they seek to change the past because they don't like the past. If an illegal immigrant actually gets citizenship, it means that it is because of a Political Left person. If you oppose giving illegal immigrants citizenship then you will be called a racist, a bigot, a xenophobe, and or a white supremacist. These attacks by the Political Left are just empty threats as they can't think of anything else. It is purely propaganda. Illegal immigrants must understand citizenship is only granted to those legal residents of another country who arrive here legally.

And then there is the issue of crime, drugs, and deportation, which is something that is part of an important issue. And yet, the Political Left hates people being deported because they believe it is against human rights. Now, deportation is a topic that seems very controversial, but it is not, as illegal immigrants have committed a crime of illegally crossing into the US border. But, if you listen to the Political Left, they say illegal immigrants should not be deported, as they could face persecution in their home country. A person by the name of Pablo Alvarado believes it is morally wrong to send illegal immigrants who have committed rape and murder back to their home country, as he believes it is just racist.[196] Yet, this is what you keep on getting from the Political Left, that sending back illegal immigrants who commit criminal acts is racist. What a bunch of hogwash. It is not racist to deport any illegal immigrant who committed a crime after the United States of America. It is not racist to deport any illegal immigrant even if they did not commit a crime within the United States of America. The Political Left who says it is racist to deport illegal immigrants is just delusional and is in their personal fantasyland. These Political Left people are just full of it. Further, this self-described activist who opposes deportation, even if the illegal immigrant committed a violent and or other criminal act should not be deported, as it hurts the country where they end up again.[197] The activist who opposes deportation believes no illegal immigrant should be deported because the people who live there (the illegal immigrant's country of origin) will start to leave in droves because of potential more crime.[198] He further claims that the United States of America is using Honduras and El Salvador as a penal colony to send back illegal immigrants who committed crimes.[199] Alas, the craziness from the Political Left does not end there, as

---

[196] Cyril Barnert, "No, it isn't racist to deport criminal illegal immigrants," *L.A. Times*, May 9, 2017, http://www.latimes.com/opinion/readersreact/la-ol-le-immigration-deportation-criminals-20170509-story.html.

[197] Andrea Castillo, Here's why some immigrant activists say not even criminals should be deported, *L.A. Times*, May 9, 2017, http://www.latimes.com/local/lanow/la-me-ln-activists-deportation-20170406-story.html.

[198] Ibid

[199] Ibid

another member of that faction believes that the deported illegal immigrants will end up as homeless and in poverty, but the Political Left do not actually know where the deported illegal immigrants end up.[200] And then there is another argument from the Political Left, saying that no illegal immigrant should ever be deported until the entire immigration system is fixed, implying that it should actually be suspended.[201] It is very and extremely apparent that the Political Left wants to ignore reality, as they continue to spew false truths about the majority of everything, unless they actually support it. The fact of the matter is that illegal immigration is a very important and significant issue to many Americans, and it is not good to support illegal immigration. In fact, illegal immigration is actually against the law, and if you knowingly harbor an illegal immigrant you are committing a crime; and the DNC actually was harboring at least one illegal immigrant during the 2016 election to finalize Hillary Clinton as their candidate during the Democratic National Convention located in Philadelphia, Pennsylvania.

At the same time, the Political Left does not want to listen to anyone but themselves, as they believe and think that they are the actual subject matter experts of everything. Well, they are wrong, because they want to limit other peoples' speech, as the Political Left only believes that they should have free speech. The Political Left supports an open border society just like in Europe, but in Europe it is much more of a problem, but the European problem will be

---

[200] Ibid

[201] Ibid

discussed later, as that is about a different immigration topic. Yet, by supporting this open border society in America, the Political Left also supports illegal immigration, as they believe no one is illegal. The illegal immigrants believe that they are not illegal, even though they came to America illegally by crossing into the US border by sneaking in. The very meaning of the nature of the word illegal immigrant is that it simply means that that immigrant does not have any documentation or that the documentation has expired but the immigrant still resides in the country. So, there you have it, as the illegal immigrants who cross the border illegally are actually illegal because they never came to the country illegally. The other nature of illegal immigration is not really used, as overstaying your visa makes does make you an illegal immigrant, but this meaning is not really reported much of the time because those illegal immigrants were actually once legal immigrants.

Nevertheless, deportation is party of every society, but Mexico will probably deport illegal immigrants, but then they don't like it when Donald Trump or another Republican in the United States of America supports the deportation of illegal immigrants. It is just plain hypocrisy in the sense that it is sad. But the Political Left has a double standard when it is about them, yet they continue to spew their hatred and their disinformation campaign. The fact of the matter is that deportation is a necessity if you are here illegally, as it is a matter of national security, yet many illegal immigrants actually committed criminal acts when they were here illegally. Deportation must occur, but the Political Left wants each and everyone one of the illegal immigrants to stay, because the Political Left feels it is a part of their platform protecting human rights. Well, when an illegal immigrant commits a crime, it is a human rights issue, as the potential crime can harm people, but the Political Left does not want to accept that fact.

And then there is the problem of sanctuary cities, and by this, the Political Left wants to actually protect and harbor illegal immigrants and even pay for a legal defense fund. Now, the Political Left claims that there is no such thing as a sanctuary city, but it was actually them (the Political Left) who created the term of sanctuary city, as they support the harboring of illegal immigrants. Now, a sanctuary city is simply a city and or other municipality that actually refuses to follow the law because they support illegal immigrants, yet they are usually controlled by many members of the Political Left. The Political Left insists that sanctuary cities are legal, yet they are actually illegal because it violates federal code if you knowingly harbor, protect, and or conceal any illegal immigrant, but the Political Left does not like that.[202] The reason why sanctuary cities violate federal law is because of what is stated in 8 USC Section 1324, which basically explains people who hides, conceals, and or shields anyone who is an illegal immigrant, can be held legally liable of breaking the law, and this can also apply to any government official if they ever

---

[202] Aaron Bandler, "5 Things You Need to Know About 'Sanctuary Cities'," *Daily Wire*, November 16, 2016, http://www.dailywire.com/news/10816/5-things-you-need-know-about-sanctuary-cities-aaron-bandler#.

decide to break this law.[203] Yet, when you look more closely at 8 USC Section 1324, you will find a penalty for smuggling, domestic transport of an illegal immigrant within the United States, harboring (as it was previously mentioned), and encouraging illegal immigration.[204] So, there you have it, anyone who breaks 8 USC Section 1324 can be actually be held accountable,[205] but the Political Left does not want to follow that law, as they claim that illegal immigrants did not do anything wrong. Well, there is a problem with that sentiment, which is that when they illegally crossed the border it was an illegal act. By the Political Left openly and knowingly supporting illegal immigration and sanctuary cities, it is clear they are also supporting a form of nullification, as they do not want to obey 8 USC Section 1324.[206] At the same time, Trump, conservatives, and Republicans are fighting these sanctuary cities, as they do not want to give and or grant any funding to them. Yet, even though Trump, conservatives, and the Republicans fights federal funding of the sanctuary cities and then sending in federal officials of the United

---

[203] Ibid

[204] United States Department of Justice: Office of the United States Attorneys, 1907. Title 8, U.S.C. 1324(a) Offenses, https://www.justice.gov/usam/criminal-resource-manual-1907-title-8-usc-1324a-offenses.

[205] Aaron Bandler, "5 Things You Need to Know About 'Sanctuary Cities'," *Daily Wire*, November 16, 2016, http://www.dailywire.com/news/10816/5-things-you-need-know-about-sanctuary-cities-aaron-bandler#.

[206] Ibid

States government so that those sanctuary cities will follow the law,[207] there will still be a constant battle by the Political Left and the Political Left occupied court system. So, even if Trump includes a stipulation that all sanctuary cities must comply with the federal law, the Political Left will still oppose it and will attempt to overturn that stipulation in court. At the same time, when Trump adds that stipulation requirement that all sanctuary cities must follow federal law in order to receive funding that cannot be overturned and or challenged by the Political Left, because that is part of Trump's budget. However, the Political Left might think they can overturn that stipulation once Trump budget's in signed into law, but they cannot, as it is law. Yet, you constantly see that the mayors of these sanctuary cities are complaining, but what they are complaining about is that they won't be able to break the law once that stipulation is included in Trump's budget regarding sanctuary cities and funding after the budget has been signed into law. On the other hand, since as of this writing, President's Obama 2017 budget is still in charge of the funding, the Political Left might be able to block that stipulation, as the 2017 federal budget was not crafted by Trump's team in the White House. So, the current 2017 federal budget might be a win for the Political Left, but once that stipulation is included in the 2018 federal budget and is signed into law, the Political Left cannot oppose it, as that stipulation was part of the process in order to get federal funding. So, if a sanctuary city does not follow that stipulation, then

---

[207] Ibid

they will not receive any funding at all, and by not being funded the sanctuary city will be forced to follow the law.

Nevertheless, it is important that this stipulation regarding federal funding and sanctuary cities be included in the 2018 Trump budget, but it is important in order to uphold federal law. At the same time, sanctuary cities are actually bad and dangerous, as it often and usually undermines law enforcement to uphold the law.[208] By that meaning, I mean that sanctuary cities are bad and dangerous for law enforcement because federal officials cannot do their jobs of having the illegal immigrants deported.[209] The reason why federal officials cannot do their jobs of enforcing the laws by deporting illegal immigrants is because the local officials in that sanctuary city do not want to comply with the current law.[210] So, in other words, the federal officials cannot deport the illegal immigrants, just because the local officials won't even comply with the law. This non-compliance even applies if the intended targets for deportation are gang members who are from another country, yet those gang members who were from different countries could not be deported until a crime was committed.[211] About sixty-six percent of all outstanding felony arrest warrants in the sanctuary city of Los Angeles, California consists of illegal immigrants, but when it comes to murder illegal immigrants

---

[208] Ibid

[209] Ibid

[210] Ibid

[211] Ibid

committed about ninety-five percent of that criminal offense.[212] So, it seems here that there is a problem with illegal immigrants and them committing crimes, but the Political Left does not want you to know this, and in fact they want do deny that specific notion. But wait, there's more, as in 2014, of the 9,265 illegal immigrants who were protected by sanctuary cities, about sixty-two percent of those shielded illegal immigrants had a criminal past that was significant, while 2,320 of those illegal immigrants were arrested again for committing another crime.[213] You see, there is a problem with sanctuary cities, but the Political Left wants to keep the way it is, as they want an open border society that supports illegal immigrants getting the advantage over that of US citizens and legal permanent residents. In fact, the local officials of the sanctuary cities are ignoring federal law just because of their political views, as they are part of the Political Left, but in sanctuary cities illegal immigrants are allowed to commit crimes and will then be arrested.[214] After the illegal immigrants are arrested, they might be released if they even serve a sentence at all, and this will now allow the illegal immigrants who commit crimes to stay within that specific sanctuary city to roam free and possibly to commit more crimes while released.[215] You keep on hearing that the Political Left supports the notion of sanctuary cities, as the local officials of the Political Left sanctuary cities believes it

---

[212] Ibid

[213] Ibid

[214] Ibid

[215] Ibid

will actually help prevent crime. Well, here is where they are wrong: illegal immigrants who commit crimes do not care about the rule of law, as they will continue to break the law until they do not want to break the law anymore. You will also here these Political Left local officials of the sanctuary cities that providing a sanctuary to illegal immigrants provides safety to the illegal immigrants who do not commit crimes. Well, the problem with that is the illegal immigrants who have no intention of committing crimes are scared about being caught by law enforcement for being in the United States of America illegally. The illegal immigrants who have no intention of committing any crime do not want to be caught by any type or manner of law enforcement official, no matter if they are federal or part of the local municipality. The illegal immigrants who have no intention of committing any crime are also afraid of contacting law enforcement because they might be caught and deported back to their home country. However, the Political Left will grab on to that last statement about being afraid of law enforcement because they might be deported back to their home country, but here is where the Political Left is wrong: the illegal immigrants who have no intention of committing any crimes will not report anything to law enforcement, but not because of politics, but because of possibly being caught. It does not matter if every politician is a Democrat, the illegal immigrants who have no intention of committing any crimes will not report crimes because they know they are here illegally, and the reason why these illegal immigrants who have no intention of committing any crimes do not want to report anything to law enforcement is that they just want to make it financially and to live the American dream. Yet, from the Political Left, you will only hear that illegal immigrants are afraid of reporting crimes because of possible retaliation from law enforcement by being deported to their home country. The Political Left is trying to play everything to their base, as they want an open border society. The reason why the illegal immigrants who have no intention of committing crimes do not want to go to law enforcement to report a crime is simply because they don't want to encounter any type of drama, meaning they have more important things to do like paying for food and earning a living. Yet, if any of the illegal immigrants who have no intention of committing any crimes at all does contact law enforcement, then they will do so, even though they know they could face potential deportation, but the illegal immigrant might try to make a deal or by trying to report the crime anonymously. The Political Left does not get it, and they will never learn about how to impose good immigration policy. When you hear someone from the Political Left explaining immigration policy, you will hear nothing but nonsense and craziness.

It is apparent that sanctuary cities are not following the law, as they are run and supported by the Political Left, who openly supports the idea of an open border society in order to support a changing society that wants to abolish the traditional founding values of a country. You see, the Political Left does not like tradition, as they want to change history by pretending it never happened. The Political Left opposes any deportation efforts of illegal immigrants, even if they committed very violent, aggressive criminal acts. It is just surprising that the Political Left wants to oppose federal law, yet they will never learn the truth about their mistakes. It is a fact that sanctuary cities see an uptick in crime, and illegal immigrants believe they can get away with anything, but in reality, there is an underground economy.[216] Sure, it sounds like it correct, because illegal immigrants consist of many violent and non-violent criminals who have no regard for the law, as they believe they are immune from everything. The Political Left does not care about what illegal immigrants do, as the Political Left believes it is the action of what they call police brutality. Well, police brutality exists, but it is being over exaggerated by the media and the Political Left. Police brutality is not that relevant in the discussion about immigration policy, as the focus should be on reforming current immigration policy by establishing new laws, as well as enforcing current laws.

This is the reason why we need anti-sanctuary city bills, in order to prevent illegal immigration. If violent criminal illegal immigrants were actually held accountable, then America would not have this problem; but time and time again, an innocent person gets killed because of just one illegal immigrant who committed a crime not once, but multiple times, and in fact they were deported many times before. But when you tell the Political Left that, they deny it and say they feel sorry. But when you try to get a law pass to end sanctuary cities, to prevent funding from going to sanctuary cities, and or to institute harsher penalties, you will get attacked by the Political Left for being anti-immigration. Well now, conservatives and

---

[216] Ibid

Republicans tried to pass something known as Kate's Law, but it was blocked by former Senator Harry Reid. Now, Kate's Law was something promoted by former Fox News host Bill O'Reilly who was only terminated because of a Media Matters campaign to spread false truths. Nevertheless, the Political Left, including Media Matters, did not like O'Reilly, so they got him hired. To get back to the point, Kate's Law would provide stricter penalties, and it reportedly being revived again as of this writing. Kate's Law, or S. 2193, which is formally known as the Stop Illegal Reentry Act, was introduced by Texas Senator Ted Cruz in the 114th Congressional session during 2015 and had ten co-sponsors in the Senate.[217] Now, with Kate's Law, the mandatory minimums would be increased and or modified to punish those illegal immigrants harsher for repeated convicted offenders who attempt to enter the United States in an illegal manner.[218] Kate's Law was attacked by Political Left Senator Harry Reid, yet the Political Left does not care about Kate Steinle because they support the idea of having an open border society, while also making up false claims about the proposed law that it would target the grants of community policing.[219] On the other hand, there was a bill introduced by Senator Patrick Toomey of the state of

---

[217] U.S. Congress, Senate, *Kate's Law or Stop Illegal Reentry Act*, 114th Cong., 1st sess., Congressional Record 276, no 120, daily ed. (October 21, 2015): S.2193.

[218] Hank Berrien, "Senate Democrats KILL 'Kate's Law' Ending Funding For Sanctuary Cities," *Daily Wire*, July 7, 2016, http://www.dailywire.com/news/7287/senate-democrats-kill-kates-law-ending-funding-hank-berrien.

[219] Ibid

Pennsylvania, and he proposed in S. 3100 that the sanctuary cities will not receive any community and economic development grants if local officials refuse to comply with detainer requests.[220] Essentially, S. 3100 states that sanctuary city officials must comply with detainer requests issued by federal officials or else face funding issues, yet its main goal is to make local officials to comply with existing law.[221] So, if you explain that to the Political Left, they still won't support it, as they don't believe in border control. The Political Left does not support legal immigration. The Political Left wants to fund the legal defenses of illegal immigrants who commit crimes. It is clear that the Political Left does not want to follow existing law, and that they are already trying to obstruct federal immigration law. The Political Left does not care about safety, as they openly support in allowing any entry of illegal immigrant into the United States of America. Instead, the Political Left decides to block a good and well-intended bill that would have tried to prevent what happened to Kate Steinle.[222] Kate Steinle's death could have been prevented, but the policies of the Political Left openly supports illegal immigration and open borders, yet the true goal of the bills introduced by Toomey and Cruz were to prevent these tragic deaths from happening by punishing illegal immigrants who commit crimes in a harsher manner.[223] You think

---

[220] Ibid

[221] Ibid

[222] Ibid

[223] Ibid

that the Political Left wants to implement harsher penalties on criminals, including illegal immigrants who commit crimes, but they refuse to do so as it violates their platform of what they believe in.

When all hopes seemed lost, it was recently reported that the US Congress will revive some form of Kate's Law, but this time the law will be included in a broader border security bill that is stated to be introduce by Senator John Cornyn of Texas and House Member Michael McCaul of Texas as well.[224] The date of introducing this new version of Kate's Law is still unknown, as it is still being drafted, but because it will be part of a larger bill, it might make it more difficult for the Political Left to object to it.[225] Of course, it was a promise made by candidate Donald Trump at the time of the 2016 election season to get Kate's Law passed; it did face obstruction before by the Democrats.[226] We do not know why the Political Left opposes common sense immigration reform, but we do know that the Political Left does not like Kate's Law, as they see it harming their policies. Well now, the reason the Political Left does probably oppose Kate's Law is that they in fact actually support illegal immigration and an open border society. We already know that Kate's Law has failed as an individual piece of legislation, as the

---

[224] Jazz Shaw, "GOP taking one more run at passing Kate's Law," *Hot Air*, May 31, 2017, http://hotair.com/archives/2017/05/31/gop-taking-one-run-passing-kates-law/.

[225] Ibid

[226] Ibid

Political Left obstructed that legislation in the Senate.[227] Basically, the newer version of Kate's Law will include the five year mandatory minimum prison sentence for any illegal immigrant who was charged twice for re-entering the United States illegally through any means necessary.[228] This five year mandatory minimum prison sentence will also be implemented and applied to any illegal immigrant who has committed a crime in the past, such as a serious felony charge and have been convicted of that crime, but this would only be applied if the illegal immigrant committed a crime in the past.[229] The Political Left would they that is an ex-post facto law, but it is not, as the illegal immigrant committed the crime in the past and was convicted of such serious crimes, yet the illegal immigrant is not really held accountable, so he/she commits another serious crime. Because the illegal immigrant committed another crime after he/she has been convicted, it is that new crime that will lead to that five year mandatory minimum prison sentence.[230] The reason why the illegal immigrant is not held responsible for many of their criminal actions is because of the Political Left. So, by simply putting in that stipulation about a five year mandatory minimum prison sentence, it will be noted that illegal immigrants who commit new crimes after

---

[227] Ibid

[228] Lydia Wheeler, "Republicans look to fulfill Trump's vow on 'Kate's Law'," *The Hill*, May 31, 2017, http://thehill.com/policy/335717-republicans-look-to-fulfill-trumps-vow-on-kates-law.

[229] Ibid

[230] Ibid

they have been convicted and released will be held accountable.[231] For now, the hope of Kate's Law is optimistic.

Yet, the Political Left has another problem, but this time it is with the state of Texas. The Republican controlled legislature, has, as of this writing, passed their own version of an anti-sanctuary city law, which was signed into law by governor Greg Abbot on Sunday, May 7, 2017.[232] Now, this newly-enacted law allows law enforcement to ask any immigrant, whether legal or not, about their immigration status; but it also forces local officials, including law enforcement officials, to obey the current federal law regarding immigration and detainer requests.[233] The whole point of the Texas law is to make sure local law enforcement officials and other Texas government officials comply with the law, as in to deport any illegal immigrant deemed a risk and a threat to national security because of the crimes they committed.[234] And, if the local law enforcement officials of Texas do not comply with the law, they can be threatened or even arrested for harboring an illegal immigrant, as they refuse to hand over that illegal immigrant.[235] The Political Left has already claimed that this new Texas law will prevent protests, but that is their only excuse, as they

---

[231] Ibid

[232] David Choi, "Texas governor signs controversial bill targeting 'sanctuary cities' in the state," *Business Insider*, May 8, 2017, http://www.businessinsider.com/texas-sanctuary-cities-bill-2017-5.

[233] Ibid

[234] Ibid

[235] Ibid

can't think of anything good enough.[236] In fact, Texas is right to institute this new law, as the United States of America is a land of laws, and this also applies to Texas because that state is a part of the United States of America.[237] It is important to hold those people and officials if they try to shield and or protect illegal immigrants, but the Political Left does not seem to get that, as they always cry wolf or foul.

Some local law enforcement officials have complained about this new Texas law, but their complain or excuse is that they would have to focus more on immigration checks and border control while also saying that it will increase crime.[238] Well, the problem with that type of complaint or excuse from the Political Left is that Texas is a border state with Mexico, and by those local law enforcement officials saying that it means they don't care about border and immigration control. There are already people and members of the Political Left who are saying that the Texas law will be or is a dangerous law, as their excuse is that it requires local law enforcement to become immigration agents of the federal government of the United States of America.[239] The problem with that immigration agent excuse from the Political Left is that they will

---

[236] Ibid

[237] Ibid

[238] Ibid

[239] Nicole Prchal Svajlenka, "With S.B. 4, Texas Ignores the Lessons of Previous Anti-Immigrant Legislation," *American Progress*, May 22, 2017, https://www.americanprogress.org/issues/immigration/news/2017/05/22/432785/s-b-4-texas-ignores-lessons-previous-anti-immigrant-legislation/.

not become immigration agents, as the role of local law enforcement is to protect the law, and in the Border States it is expected that the local law enforcement officials will check immigration status. Law enforcement officials would check the immigration status of any immigrant because it is part of upholding the law. But no, the Political Left does not see it that way, as they believe it is dangerous, so they say it erodes trust and reduces public safety; yet it is clear from the Political Left that they do support illegal immigration.[240]

Nevertheless, the outrage from the Political Left due to this Texas anti-sanctuary city becoming law is insane and ridiculous, but it should not surprise you and other people. Political Left protestors have decided to protest at the Texas capitol because of the new Texas law being implemented in the future.[241] Now, when these Political Left protestors decided to interrupt the session, law enforcement had to be called in order to clear the entire gallery.[242] This protest by the Political Left also occurred on Memorial Day, one of the days America observes its members of the military, but the Political Left rather wants to protest because they do not like the constitution.[243] The Political Left protestors decided to chant out against the supporters of the new Texas law, and they even implied that the

---

[240] Ibid

[241] Brooke Singman, "Sanctuary Cities protests interrupt Texas House session," *Fox News*, May 29, 2017, http://www.foxnews.com/politics/2017/05/29/sanctuary-cities-protests-interrupt-texas-house-session.html.

[242] Ibid

[243] Ibid

politicians who voted to pass the law will be voted out of office.[244] Another well common excuse the Political Left protestors stated was that they will see you in court, implying that the Political Left will win against the state of Texas.[245] Already, you have these Political Left organizations filing frivolous lawsuits against the state of Texas saying the new Texas law is discriminatory against certain people, but this is a common tactic of the Political Left, to file lawsuits based on their hatred of the law.[246] The Political Left implies that they hate the law because they are actually against the law, the constitution, and the declaration of independence; but if a member of their own faction does something similar, well the Political Left thinks that it is constitutional. In fact, the Political Left only supports immigration laws that they impose and or institute, so to them, they have an actual double standard. At the same time, the Political Left organization bringing this lawsuit against Texas says it supports racial profiling while also stating it is unconstitutional.[247] Well, everything that the Political Left complains about has to do with this excuse of racially profiling people, and even more, when they hate it, they claim it is unconstitutional. You see, the Political Left has their own double standard, as indicated before, but they don't want to admit it. You have seen this in both of Trump's travel moratorium of certain countries, where the attorneys of the Political Left openly admit they

[244] Ibid

[245] Ibid

[246] Ibid

[247] Ibid

would have not brought a law suit if Clinton won the 2016 presidential election. It is purely a ploy because they are using a double standard. But wait, the Political Left complains about illegal immigrants being deported, and this time it is about these so-called dreamers.

Now, President Obama gave a free pass to a certain class of illegal immigrants and promised they would not be deported if they did not commit a crime or something like that. Basically, these illegal aliens or illegal immigrants are known as Dreamers, and to be eligible as a dreamer you have to be brought to the United States of America in an illegal manner when you were a child, but it applies to youth between the ages of fifteen and thirty, which is somewhat confusing because a person who is a youth is no more than twenty-five years old.[248] Anyway, if you are an eligible illegal immigrant youth, you cannot be convicted of any serious crimes, but to be eligible, you must have been brought here illegally before the age of sixteen.[249] To be eligible as a dreamer, you must also have lived in the United States of America for a minimum of five consecutive years, but you must have a high school diploma or have a GED in order to stay eligible.[250] If you are between the ages of five and fourteen, you might be

---

[248] American Immigration Council, "Who and Where the DREAMers Are, Revised Estimates," *American Immigration Council*, October 16, 2012, https://www.americanimmigrationcouncil.org/research/who-and-where-dreamers-are-revised-estimates.

[249] Ibid

[250] Ibid

eligible, but you need to meet all of the current requirements.[251] If you are between the ages of fifteen and thirty and do not have a high school diploma, you can qualify if you have a GED.[252] Now, this deferred action can be renewed every two years, but if you do not meet the requirements or if you break the law by having and or getting a criminal of at least one felony, any type of significant misdemeanor, and or at least three misdemeanors, then you will become eligible for deportation.[253] So, you might think that this deferred action for illegal immigrants is good, but you are actually wrong, because it was actually a bad policy.

The reason why this Dreamer policy is bad is because many of these alleged Dreamers have actually been arrested for crimes. For instance, at least three Dreamers were arrested by federal immigration officials for being involved in gang-related activity.[254] It has already been revealed as of this writing that at least 1,500 and above have had their protected Dreamer status revoked because they were involved in gang-related activities or even committed crimes.[255] There you have it, the program enacted by Obama has actually caught many illegal immigrants who should have never been admitted to the program,

---

[251] Ibid

[252] Ibid

[253] Ibid

[254] John Binder, "DREAMers Arrested in Nationwide Gang Crackdown," *Breitbart*, May 11, 2017, http://www.breitbart.com/texas/2017/05/11/dreamers-arrested-nationwide-gang-crackdown/.

[255] Ibid

but the Political Left refuses to accept that. The Political Left believes it is a necessary program because they support open borders and illegal immigration, yet they have no respect for the constitution and always make excuses for their flawed reasoning. And then you have this case of Jessica Colotl, which is part of the broader problem. Anyways, the case of Jessica Colotl is interesting, as this illegal immigrant was stated to be the poster-child to support the open border society people.[256] So, in other words, it seems that Jessica Colotl was the original Dreamer; but if that isn't enough, the Political Left basically used her to advance their narrative of supporting illegal immigration and an open border society, but now the entire Political Left is frustrated that Jessica Colotl will be deported back to Mexico.[257] Now, let's look closer at this Jessica Colotl case, as the reason she is being deported back to Mexico is that she committed crimes, and the Department of Homeland Security even cited her own criminal history for the basis of deportation.[258] It is interesting that this illegal immigrant actually became a Dreamer, because she got caught by law enforcement officials for driving without a license in 2010.[259] And in 2011, Jessica Colotl admitted guilt and entered into a no contest guilty plea to a felony charge to law enforcement

[256] John Binder, "Arrest Record Puts Activist DREAMer on 'Priority' Deportation List," *Breitbart*, May 12, 2017, http://www.breitbart.com/texas/2017/05/12/arrest-record-puts-activist-dreamer-priority-deportation-list/.

[257] Ibid

[258] Ibid

[259] Ibid

officials in Georgia for making up false statements under oath, according to previous reports.[260] Because Jessica Colotl pleaded guilty to a felony charge for lying to law enforcement officials, it actually means that she is eligible for deportation, according to reports.[261] So, let's look at her case here, because she was not eligible to receive DACA status, as she openly admitted guilt to making false statements;[262] and for an illegal immigrant youth to be eligible for DACA status, they can't commit specific types or classes of crimes.[263] If you remember this DACA policy, it went into effect under the Obama administration, during August 15, 2012.[264] Yet, how Jessica Colotl was eligible for DACA status, well the Political Left cites that the guilty plea was actually part of a diversion program and that they say she never made a false statement to law enforcement officials.[265] Yet, the Political Left falsely claims that Jessica Colotl never made a false statement and that the case was dismissed, but that is entirely

---

[260] Ibid

[261] Ibid

[262] Ibid

[263] Immigration Equality, DACA (Deferred Action for Childhood Arrivals), http://www.immigrationequality.org/get-legal-help/our-legal-resources/path-to-status-in-the-u-s/daca-deferred-action-for-childhood-arrivals/.

[264] Ibid

[265] American Civil Liberties Union, ACLU takes legal action to restore DACA protections for Dreamer in Georgia, *American Civil Liberties Union*, May 23, 2017, https://www.aclu.org/news/aclu-takes-legal-action-restore-daca-protections-dreamer-georgia.

false on the merits.[266] Jessica Colotl was found guilty of driving without a license by a jury in 2010, and in 2011 she was indicted for making false statements to law enforcement.[267] But in 2013, the felony charge was dismissed, only because someone from the Political Left thought it was a good idea for a diversion program, even though the court and the Sheriff's office that the diversion program was not actually appropriate for this specific case.[268] Even the newly-elected district attorney had a problem with this diversion program, as now he made it possible that illegal immigrants would not be allowed to take part in any diversion program of the type.[269] Let's be clear here, Jessica Colotl was convicted by a jury in Georgia in 2010 for driving without a license, and this does make it a significant crime because illegal immigrants are not supposed to drive a motor vehicle.[270]

Further, the only reason the felony charge was dismissed is due to the matter that a Political Left district attorney or some district attorney who supports the Political Left decided it was appropriate for Jessica Colotl to enter into a pre-trial diversion program.[271] But,

---

[266] Ibid

[267] Andria Simmons, "Charge against Jessica Colotl dropped," *Atlanta Journal Constitution*, January 10, 2013, http://www.ajc.com/news/charge-against-jessica-colotl-dropped/yj5PpLBUAcWiIIol2IIengK/.

[268] Ibid

[269] Ibid

[270] Ibid

[271] Ibid

even though Jessica Colotl entered into a diversion program, she made false statements to law enforcement, and law enforcement officials found that Jessica Colotl provided inaccurate information, so it basically means that she indeed committed a crime.[272] But, the diversion program is still a guilty plea, as it required 150 community service hours, yet the only reason the felony charge was dismissed was to protect her, and the people who wanted to protect her was the Political Left.[273] In fact, it is considered a significant misdemeanor to be convicted for driving without a license,[274] and that should be a basis for Jessica Colotl to be deported and her DACA status rescinded, as no illegal immigrant should be able to drive without a license. Yet, the Political Left does not see it that way, as they believe illegal immigrants should be able to drive, and this has been implemented in the communist and socialist state of California.[275] The Political Left just wants to support illegal immigrants, as they feel illegal immigrants are actually legal residents of the entire United States of America. Well, the state of California and the rest of the Political Left are delusional, as they don't care about the safety about

---

[272] Ibid

[273] Ibid

[274] John Binder, "Arrest Record Puts Activist DREAMer on 'Priority' Deportation List," *Breitbart*, May 12, 2017, http://www.breitbart.com/texas/2017/05/12/arrest-record-puts-activist-dreamer-priority-deportation-list/.

[275] Tatiana Sanchez, "DMV licensed 800,000 undocumented immigrants under 2-year-old law," *Mercury News*, December 28, 2016, updated December 30, 2016, http://www.mercurynews.com/2016/12/28/dmv-licensed-800000-undocumented-immigrants-under-2-year-old-law/.

other people, yet this is due to their view that they believe an open
border society is good. It should be noted that President Trump, the
conservatives, and the Republicans are trying to prevent illegal
immigration, but the Political Left will oppose everything, as the
Political Left openly supports an open society and they believe that
illegal immigration is good.

Nevertheless, any type of misdemeanor can be considered as
a significant misdemeanor, if an illegal immigrant was "sentenced to
time in custody of more than 90 days," yet this does not include any
type of suspended sentence or even "time served beyond the
sentence while under an immigration hold."[276] Even though the jail or
prison sentence was less than ninety days, the U.S. Citizenship and
Immigration Services still retains the appropriate discretion to view
the misdemeanor as something that is significant, meaning they can
still deny and or revoke the DACA application.[277] At the same time,
Jessica Colotl was only sentenced to three days in jail for driving
without a license, but she was also had to serve "11 months and 27
days on probation."[278] But, the Political Left does not want you to
know this, as they actually want to bury this type of information. Any
illegal immigrant who drives without a license should be found guilty

---

[276] NOLO, When Significant Misdemeanors Bar DACA Eligibility,
http://www.nolo.com/legal-encyclopedia/significant-misdemeanors-affect-daca-
eligibility.html.

[277] Ibid

[278] Andria Simmons, "Charge against Jessica Colotl dropped," *Atlanta
Journal Constitution*, January 10, 2013, http://www.ajc.com/news/charge-
against-jessica-colotl-dropped/yj5PpLBUAcWiIIol2HengK/.

of a significant misdemeanor but to become tough on immigration, illegal immigrants should not be allowed to drive at all. But the fact that Jessica Colotl received a light jail or prison sentence tells you something, yet it was not so light because she still had to serve nearly a year on probation.[279] The probation that was required of Jessica Colotl is actually significant, as it is actually harsher of a sentence than her three day jail sentence.[280] And since there is a significant difference between the probation sentence and the actual jail sentence,[281] there is a possibility that the United States government will see that as significant because they retain the appropriate discretion to determine if it is actually a significant crime.[282] But, the Political Left does not want to deport anyone, as they think it is part of inclusion, tolerance, and acceptance, yet they forget a ton of those illegal aliens and or illegal immigrants actually commit crimes. It is simply a ploy by the Political Left to change and destroy the history of the United States of America because the Political Left hates the past, but they also believe that illegal immigration is not against the law, as they are living in their personal own fantasy land. The Political Left wants to destroy the entire past and replace it with values that do not match with the traditional founding values of a country.

---

[279] Ibid

[280] Ibid

[281] Ibid

[282] NOLO, When Significant Misdemeanors Bar DACA Eligibility, http://www.nolo.com/legal-encyclopedia/significant-misdemeanors-affect-daca-eligibility.html.

At the same time, the Political Left wants to destroy and then change the history and traditional values of the United States of America, and they have already done this in Europe, but even in Europe the Political Left is delusional about what is happening in their countries. This is common practice now by the Political Left in Europe, as they do not support the traditional founding values of a country, but instead they want to replace it with values that support fear and Sharia Law. It is a fact that there are certain places within the United States of America that support Sharia Law, yet reasons could be unknown or it could be due to the fact that the Political Left does not care about the safety of the American people. In one place of the United States of America, some person is trying to enforce Sharia Law, and this is said to be happening Minneapolis, Minnesota, in which the person is making all kinds of demands in support of Sharia, yet for some reason CAIR and the rest of the Muslim community does not like this outsider, implying that they oppose Sharia Law.[283] But then you have CAIR actually supporting Sharia Law because they believe it should not be banned in the United States of America, saying the ban violates the establishment clause, but it does not violate the establishment clause.[284] The reason why

---

[283] Kerry Picket, "Local Muslims Try To Shut Down Sharia Law Patrol In Minneapolis Neighborhood," *Daily Caller*, April 14, 2017, http://dailycaller.com/2017/04/14/local-muslims-try-to-shut-down-sharia-law-patrol-in-minneapolis-neighborhood/.

[284] Billy Hallowell, "Muslim Group Seeks to Ban Sharia Law in America," *The Blaze*, September 13, 2011, http://www.theblaze.com/news/2011/09/13/muslim-group-seeks-to-ban-sharia-law-in-america/.

the Sharia Law ban does not violate the establishment clause is that it attempts to ban a law that is a violation of the United States of America, as Sharia Law actually enforces harsh penalties based on religion, and in the United States of America, religion is never part of the law and the constitution. Any law that imposes religion as the basis for punishment is unconstitutional and it violates the traditional and the founding values of the United States of America. But the Political Left will ignore that and say that the constitution does not matter, because they believe the constitutional is a living document. Yet, the Political Left is delusional, as now they are trying to the same thing in Europe, but this time it is about refugees.

In Europe, there is a problem of migrants and or refugees assimilating into their new and or temporary home, and this has been widely documented. The proper name of the European problem can be referred to as the European migrant crisis, which can also be referred as the European refugee crisis, because there was an influx of migrants going to the continent of Europe.[285] Now, this migration or refugee crisis occurred in the year of 2015, when one-million and above refugees and other types of migrants decided to go to Europe, which then caused an influx of too many people, and this further increased tensions within the European Union.[286] Now, the problem with this influx of too many migrants and refugees going to Europe

---

[285] Wikipedia, European migrant crisis, https://en.wikipedia.org/wiki/European_migrant_crisis#cite_note-13.

[286] BBC, "Migrant crisis: Migration to Europe explained in seven charts," *British Broadcasting Corporation*, March 4, 2016, http://www.bbc.com/news/world-europe-34131911.

is that there is a disagreement of how to resettle these people;[287] and many politicians became outraged of these same migrants and refugees committing crimes, but then the politicians who demanded that this mass migration stop, well they were called racist, xenophobic, Islamaphobic, misogynists, bigots, and other political name slurs, but the people who are calling these politicians these names are also part of the Political Left. The Political Left, especially in Europe, do not like it when someone demands more scrutiny and vetting, as these are the same politicians and members of the Political Left that support open borders. Besides the fact, the reason of why this mass migration occurs is due to the matter of what has occurred in Syria, Afghanistan, and Iraq for the most part, but there were also migrants and or refugees from Kosovo, Pakistan, Albania, Eritrea, Nigeria, Ukraine, and Iran.[288] Yet, the problem of what has occurred in Syria was one of the main driving factors for this mass migration problem.[289] Many of these migrants and or refugees who actually arrived in Europe actually declared asylum, but almost 500,000 chose to claim asylum in Germany, yet this number has been understated, since the government indicated a little over one million people.[290] Now, the majority of these migrants and or refugees arrived to the continent of Europe via sea while just fewer than 35,000 arrived via

---

[287] Ibid

[288] Ibid

[289] Ibid

[290] Ibid

land.[291] Many of these migrants have died, as the journey was dangerous and very unsafe, yet tensions within the European Union have increased because of how to resettle the migrants.[292]

Nevertheless, this mass migration crisis has caused tensions to increase amongst many politicians, as previously indicated, within the European Union. In France, Marine Le Pen, a candidate for the 2017 French presidential election, demanded that the French government restore the national borders because of a terrorist attack.[293] Marine Le Pen, Nigel Farage, Beppe Grillo, Geert Wilders, and several other European politicians have either called for the end of the Schengen area agreement or to review it in order to determine if it is actually a good idea to have an open border society, and the reason why is due to the fact that the migrants and or refugees are taking advantage of the open border system.[294] It is true that this migrant and or refugee crisis has made Europe a more violent environment, as terrorists have actually infiltrated the refugees and migrants by posing as refugees and or migrants, yet the reason for this happening is due to the fact that the Political Left in Europe

---

[291] Ibid

[292] Ibid

[293] Sam Meredith, "Le Pen calls for government to immediately reinstate French borders after Paris attack," *CNBC*, April 21, 2017, http://www.cnbc.com/2017/04/21/le-pen-calls-reinstate-french-borders-attack.html.

[294] Kim Willsher, "European far right calls for end to open borders after Berlin suspect shot," *The Guardian*, December 23, 2016, https://www.theguardian.com/world/2016/dec/23/european-far-right-end-to-open-borders-schengen-berlin-le-pen.

supports an open border society.[295] Because of this refugee crisis, crime has increased in Europe, where the refugees resort to raping women, committing terrorist attacks by driving down people using vehicles, and destroying the personal property of people and businesses.[296] Yet, there is also the problem of the Political Left implementing Sharia Law into certain parts of Europe, just because of this refugee crisis, as many of these refugees seem intolerant of other religious views, and this implies there is an assimilation problem with many of these refugees.[297]

At the same time, you thought that the Political Left will support harsher laws because of this refugee crisis, but no, because the Political Left decided to attack and protest Sweden's new laws regarding seeking asylum.[298] The Political Left are angered by Sweden's new laws on asylum because children asylum seekers have to now prove that they are actually children, that the amount of refugees admitted to Sweden are limited to be more manageable, and that refugees can only stay and apply for a three year period.[299] Well,

---

[295] Rachel Alexander, "Europe Reaping What it Sowed With Open Borders Policy for Muslim Refugees," *Town Hall*, December 27, 2016, https://townhall.com/columnists/rachelalexander/2016/12/27/europe-reaping-what-it-sowed-with-open-borders-policy-for-muslim-refugees-n2263851.

[296] Ibid

[297] Ibid

[298] Caroline Mortimer, "Laws restricting refugees' rights in Sweden spark backlash as thousands take to the streets," *Independent*, October 23, 2016, http://www.independent.co.uk/news/world/europe/refugee-crisis-sweden-new-law-restrict-asylum-claims-child-migrants-afghanistan-a7376656.html.

[299] Ibid

the problem that the Political Left has issues with is probably that refugees will no longer be able to gain permanent residency, and instead, the residential permit will only be for a temporary three-year stay.[300] This just tells you that the Political Left does not like good reform, and they even support refugees being issued a permanent residency permit, as the Political Left does not like the idea that the new law would only provide a three-year residency permit.[301] The Political Left will never learn, but just when they try to attack good and reasonable reform, another attack by a refugee occurs, but they (the Political Left) still cannot comprehend the problem of their failed and outdated policies. This time, a seventeen year-old refugee from the country of Afghanistan raped and killed a medical student in Germany, which is home to Angela Merkel's failed open border policy.[302] Now, for good reason, this child refugee was arrested, which was very fortunate indeed, but the Political Left strikes back by saying don't blame every refugee from Afghanistan, Iraq, and or Syria because it makes it unfair to them.[303] Yet, the Political Left still does not comprehend, as the majority of the refugees who commit those crimes in Europe are either from Afghanistan, Iraq, and or Syria. In Germany, the Political Left or the people who support an open

[300] Ibid

[301] Ibid

[302] Erik Kirschbaum, "Arrest of refugee in rape and slaying in Germany threatens Merkel's immigration policy," *L.A. Times*, December 5, 2016, http://www.latimes.com/world/europe/la-fg-germany-refugee-murder-20161205-story.html.

[303] Ibid

border society, well they want to silence the opposition, as they want to avoid the truth by saying it is all fine and dandy, yet this includes the blocking of comments.[304] And, if you want to control the national borders and implement a better policy that supports safety, you will be certainly called a racist, xenophobic, Islamaphobic, and or a bigot by the Political Left, as the reasoning of the Political Left is that you must accept them because of their clear support for open borders for everyone.[305] In fact many Muslims do integrate well in society, but the Political Left is trying to hide the fact that many more Muslims cannot really integrate and or assimilate into western countries, and the reason why might be due to the potential influence from Islamist groups.[306] The Muslims who migrate to the West are told to form a parallel society and to keep mentioning that the West and Islam are in a constant war.[307] According to Islam, there is a view that government should be connected with religion, and this could be a potential factor of why Muslims are having problems with their new Western host countries, as they don't want to accept the new values of their new home country.[308] At the same, this problem of accepting the new values of their home countries means that there will be a

---

[304] Ibid

[305] Megan G. Oprea, "Don't Compare U.S. Immigration To Europe's Migrant Crisis," *The Federalist*, September 30, 2016, http://thefederalist.com/2016/09/30/dont-compare-us-immigration-europes-migrant-crisis/.

[306] Ibid

[307] Ibid

[308] Ibid

cultural clash, as the Western countries don't restrict the freedom and the dress of women.[309] Another problem is that many Muslims have with the West is the fact that they support Sharia Law, and by supporting Sharia Law, many Muslims will often view Western Laws as the enemy, which means it will lead to a cultural clash.[310] But, the Political Left does not really care about that, as they believe Islam is a religion of peace, yet while it could be a religion of peace, many Muslims have problems with Western society because of Western values, Western culture, and of Western beliefs. Instead of wanting to assimilate and or to integrate into a new home country, many Muslims seek to follow Sharia Law, and by doing this, many of those Muslims refuse to accept and adopt Western culture, Western values, and Western beliefs. Yet, the Political Left still does not get it, as they believe that the traditional founding values and beliefs are the problem. However, the traditional founding values and beliefs of a society is what makes a country great and unique, yet the Political Left wants to replace those traditional founding values and beliefs that supports radical extremist views that promote anti-social behavior. There is a problem with this radical extremist view of Political Leftists, as their behavior promotes radicalism, extremism, communism, fascism, Marxism, socialism, and anti-social behavior. In other words, the Political Left supports breaking the law, as they do not like people of opposing views. Even though the Political Lefts says they are tolerant and supports inclusiveness, they are actually

---

[309] Ibid

[310] Ibid

not, as they constantly support and engage in fascism, anarchism, violence, aggression, and many other criminal acts. And when you try to institute a limit of the number of migrants or refugees into a country, you are called a racist, a misogynist, an Islamophobe, a xenophobe, a bigot, and some other political name slur by the Political Left. It is simply amazing that they are promoting their views, as the views and beliefs of the Political Left are to destroy and change history by avoiding the past. You can't argue or talk to the Political Left in an open debate, as they will attempt to shut you down because the Political Left does not like your views, your values, and or your opinions. On the other hand, it is expected that they never listen, and so Muslim migrants in many Political Left European countries seem to get a pass.

When I mean pass, well, special areas or neighborhoods in many European countries have something known as No Go Zones, which are basically specific areas that are deemed too dangerous if the person has no police protection.[311] These No Go Zones have been confirmed, and from one perspective, it was confirmed by the person in charge of an ambulance union in Sweden; yet to them, a No Go Zone actually means that they cannot enter those specific areas because they are just too dangerous to enter.[312] At the same time, these No Go Zones are a bad idea, as it seems to isolate specific

---

[311] Larry O'Connor, "VIDEO: Head of Ambulance Union Confirms 'No-Go Zones' in Sweden," *Weekly Standard*, February 27, 2017, http://www.weeklystandard.com/video-head-of-ambulance-union-confirms-no-go-zones-in-sweden/article/2007000.

[312] Ibid

nationalities, as they do not want to integrate into society. So, from my perspective, a No Go Zone actually is basically a bad idea, as it promotes the idea of terrorism and other types of anti-social crime, as No Go Zones are too dangerous to enter; and due to the fact that the people living in those No Go Zones will attempt to commit crimes against people if you are not from that area, a person and or their vehicle not from that area might be assaulted with objects and weapons.[313] In Germany, it is basically the same thing, as there are also No Go Zones; and specifically No Go Zones can be described as lawless areas.[314] If law enforcement or outsiders even try to go to these No Go Zones, then they might be attacked by the migrants who live in those areas.[315] Migrants and refugees are basically preventing people from going into these areas known as No Go Zones, and before they were even No Go Zones, they were once considered vibrant and possibly very up-scale neighborhoods or areas.[316] But with the event of this mass migration crisis in Europe, law enforcement has been unable to control these neighborhoods that are now known as No Go Zones because of the chaotic atmosphere.[317] Nevertheless, the reason why these No Go Zones

---

[313] Ibid

[314] Zoie O'Brien, "GERMANY NO-GO ZONES: Police afraid to go into lawless areas after open-door immigration," *Express*, November 8, 2016, http://www.express.co.uk/news/world/729782/Germany-no-go-police-afraid-lawless-areas-migrants-rule.

[315] Ibid

[316] Ibid

[317] Ibid

exist is because of the Political Left and their failed policy of supporting an open border society; but then what actually causes terrorism, well the Political Left says it is due to climate change, but that is false, so it is important to point out the fact that Political Left policy is bad and dangerous.

As you can see, the Political Left sees climate change as the true cause of terrorism, but this is actually false, as terrorists often commit their terrorist acts because they do not agree with the West. Now, to get to the point, the rest of this chapter shall discuss climate change and how the Political Left distorts reality. Now, climate change is a natural cycle of the environmental process, and without this natural cycle of climate change then the environment will actually be extremely unsafe and dangerous, but the Political Left does not want you to know that. You see, the Political Left blames humans and fabricated evidence that promotes extreme regulations. Yet, the Political Left likes to always say that climate change is the same as global warming, so if they want to say it like that, let's look at the meaning behind global warming meaning climate change and vice versa. Or so you thought, as the Political Left basically believes that global warming and climate change are the same thing, as they contribute one as the same, as they believe that humans are the only reason why the planet to them is being destroyed. But let's get serious, humans are not the main factor hurting and or destroying the planet Earth, as the Political Left just wants to blame everything on other factors.

In fact, the idea of global warming actually "refers to the global-average temperature increase that has been observed over the last one hundred years or more."[318] Now, look at that statement closely, and you might have guessed that the Political Left will use it to their advantage, by saying that the thing responsible for that warming is humans, yet not much research has been conducted to determine the causes of natural mechanisms of global warming, and that is why the Political Left likes to blame everything on humans regarding the changing climate.[319] So, instead of conducting additional research, the Political Left decides that humans are the main cause or contributor to climate change, yet global warming or climate change is entirely natural, but the Political Left would want to say otherwise.[320] Let's examine climate change more closely and how the Political Left is wrong on the issue. Evidence does suggest that global warming or climate change is a natural process and this indicates it is a natural cycle, yet the evidence indicates that the climate system is not really sensitive to aerosol pollution and greenhouse gas emissions from humans.[321] So, if the climate or atmosphere is not really sensitive from emissions or aerosol pollution, then why do the Political Left saying climate change is

---

[318] Roy Spencer, "Global Warming: Natural or Manmade,?" Roy Spencer PhD Global Warming Blog, http://www.drroyspencer.com/global-warming-natural-or-manmade/.

[319] Ibid

[320] Ibid

[321] Ibid

manmade, well the problem is that the Political Left does not research the actual problem and instead seeks to look at something outdated.[322] Even if the Political Left claims they know the actual sensitivity of the climate, they are not telling the truth as the Political Left most likely misinterpreted the entire process.[323] Yet, the Political Left still does not want to believe climate change is a natural cycle or process, but evidence suggest that the climate system itself is actually causing the climate to change, and the chaotic fluctuations or any fluctuations at all in the atmosphere and the oceans can potentially change the cloudiness average globally.[324] But, these chaotic fluctuations are not that large, as they are actually small, and all it takes is one small change that will change the actual climate system, as any small change in the climate can change the climate significantly.[325] On the other hand, the Political Left will try to dispute this and try to say that CO2 or carbon dioxide is the main factor behind climate change and or the problem they call global warming. However, an industrial chemist says that carbon dioxide is not the cause of global warming and or climate change, as thermodynamics say it is nearly impossible.[326] And yet, there is

---

[322] Ibid

[323] Ibid

[324] Ibid

[325] Ibid

[326] Mark Imisides, "Chemistry Expert: Carbon Dioxide Can't Cause Global Warming," *Principia-Scientific*, February 9, 2017, http://principia-scientific.org/chemistry-expert-carbon-dioxide-cant-cause-global-warming/.

another problem with the Political Left's take on climate change or what they call global warming, and this is because planet Earth is tilted on an axis, and the tilting of the axis actually determines the seasons of each continent.[327]

Further, whenever the southern portion of the hemisphere is tilted towards the sun, then there is more direct sunlight during the day and the days are actually longer.[328] Yet, when the southern portion of the hemisphere is tilted away from the sun it is the exact opposite, as now there is less direct sunlight causing the days to be shorter.[329] The Political Left would like you to ignore that. However, when there is more direct sunlight then it would be lead to hotter temperatures, and in the summer the temperatures are actually hotter because of this direct sunlight.[330] When there is less direct sunlight, then it is cooler, which means temperatures would be colder, and this would be the case for winter seasons, as people would use heaters to keep warm.[331] So, the basic and logically reasoning is that winter is cold and summer is hot,[332] yet the Political Left does not care about this because they say the winter months were hotter than average. The fact of the matter is that some places are hot because they are

---

[327] Ibid

[328] Ibid

[329] Ibid

[330] Ibid

[331] Ibid

[332] Ibid

too close to the equator while other places actually don't receive any cold and or even hot weather. Yet, there is still this false claim that ninety-seven percent of all climate scientists say that they agree with climate change and it is manmade, but here is where they are wrong: it is a misrepresentation of the facts and the percentage of climate scientists never actually stated that climate change was caused by humans.[333] This ninety-seven percent claim is clearly inaccurate and misleading, and it is probably and most likely due to some specific ideology with a purpose; but even if this claim has and was disproven and discredited, they still cite it as fact.[334] And then the same Political Left cites that icebergs are melting away, but for that purpose, they believe the icebergs will never return, but that is actually false and misleading, as ice does melt and that is because of the sun. So, it is rather foolish of the Political Left to say it melts, but really it is actually due to the sun. And for their disappearance myth, well ice is supposed to melt because of the sun, even though you might not be able to see the sun. On another note, the Political Left is now trying to label their global cooling nonsense claim between the 1960s and the 1970s as a myth.[335] The Political Left's global cooling claim

---

[333] Alex Epstein, "97% Of Climate Scientists Agree Is 100% Wrong," *Forbes*, January 6, 2015, https://www.forbes.com/sites/alexepstein/2015/01/06/97-of-climate-scientists-agree-is-100-wrong/2/#1210523f3414.

[334] Ibid

[335] James Delingpole, "Massive Cover-Up Exposed: Lying Alarmists Rebranded 70s Global Cooling Scare as a Myth," *Breitbart*, September 14, 2016, http://www.breitbart.com/london/2016/09/14/massive-cover-exposed-lying-alarmists-rebranded-70s-global-cooling-scare-myth/.

nonsense cites that an overwhelming eighty-six percent of the scientific community indicated that the planet Earth was on the verge of a global cooling scare, but now the same Political Left is saying that this consensus had very little support in the scientific community.[336] Well, it looks like a cover up because it is a cover up, as the Political Left wants to hide what they said decades before, but they can't hide anymore as someone by the name of Kenneth Richard has caught the Political Left.[337] The reason why I believe the Political Left is trying to cover up their global cooling scare claim is that they now support their nonsense claim of global warming, and the Political Left will just keep trying to change their opinions, as they have no real facts. On the other hand, there is this smog problem, but smog does not really warm or cool the planet, as all it creates is a toxic and unlivable environments; and when such the environment is considered toxic, people need to wear masks, but clearly, the Political Left has lost it.

As a matter of fact, global warming and global cooling is a myth, as the Political Left wants to claim it is bad for the planet. But in reality, it is normal for the planet Earth to cool and warm as she pleases, as there is a natural cycle known as climate change. Climate change is a natural cycle because everything does fluctuate from time to time, as this is normal to protect the climate and the rest of the environment, in order to protect the Earth from melting and or from another ice age. But the Political Left does not want you to know

---

[336] Ibid

[337] Ibid

that, as they want to blame humans, as the Political Left hates coal. And, as a matter of fact, Hillary Clinton did state that she wanted to get rid of coal mining jobs, but then she stated that her comments were mischaracterized and taken out of context, even though her comments were not taken out of context, as she was very clear in her words and reasoning. The Political Left thinks that solar and wind energy should replace coal because it is cleaner than coal, but coal is cleaner than ever while solar and wind energy costs too much money. Nevertheless, the Political Left wants to create a false and unproven narrative, as their goal is to ignore the past. Yet, when they argue against borders, they are implying that illegal immigration is a good idea and that love can end terrorism. The fact of the matter is that the Political Left does not want to conduct new research regarding the climate, but if they do conduct new climate research then they would probably manipulate their results to suggest a false narrative, as they are the Political Left.

After all, the Political Left believes that they have the only actual and factual arguments, but the majority of their arguments are either false and or misleading. The Political Left constantly believes that they are right and everyone else is wrong, so they make up false claims. In any matter, immigration is a problem and it needs to get under control by implementing better policies, new and harsher laws for illegal aliens who commit crimes, and provide for a protection barrier such as a new border wall that will keep out illegal immigrants and drugs. Nevertheless, the Political Left will ignore this idea and claim it is racist, xenophobic, bigotry, hatred, and misogynist. The

Political Left needs to be educated in a better manner regarding immigration and the climate, but they will probably never happen, as they are just full of it.

A Chapter Five

Government Abuse and Overregulation

N ow, this chapter is mainly about government

abusing their authority, such as government abusing their power by abusing the law and or the constitution, as well as miscellaneous actions of the Political Left. This chapter will include gun control, climate change denial persecution, environmental terrorism, and other issues. The Political Left has constantly attacked civil liberties, as they supported slavery, and were the main reason why a civil war actually started. Now, the Political Left in the southern states said it was a matter of states' right, but the other issue was that they still supported slavery. However, when you confront them regarding the past, the Political Left will stay it never existed in that way or you are making it up. In fact, the Political Left doesn't want to admit their horrible past because they want to change it. In other words, the Political Left wants to make something up, and so they will distort reality.

Nevertheless, that is not the worst of the Political Left, as the worse of it is to abuse the constitution of the United States of America by falsely saying it is a living document. Another way the Political Left abuses their authority is that they try to prosecute or persecute you if you do not have their same ideology. Lastly, the Political Left likes to overstep the boundaries of the law, as they believe the constitution is obsolete. As a matter of fact, this was proven time and time again, but one of the most well-known claims of government abuse by the Political Left is to take away the guns away of everyday innocent American citizens by usurping the second amendment. Now, the Political Left supports gun control because they do not like guns, yet they are also misinformed. Controlling guns is a federal issue, as the second amendment in the bill of rights of the constitution actually makes owning and having a gun a constitutional right. Yet, the Political Left hates the second amendment, so they try to pass restrictive and unconstitutional laws. The reason why the Political Left likes gun control is that it makes them believe that a new law will make it safer to protect people from gun violence, yet this reasoning is flawed.[338] And for another reason, the Political

---

[338] Chad Stafko, "Real Reasons Liberals Hate Guns," *Red State*, January 16, 2013, http://www.redstate.com/diary/stafko/2013/01/16/real-reasons-liberals-hate-guns/.

Left believes gun control is good because it will prevent another senseless killing, yet their reasoning for this is that gun control is good because it will help end the violence. Well, the Political Left believes they should determine who owns guns because they think and believe that people should not be able to make decisions on their own.[339] Every time there is a tragic shooting, the Political Left cites more gun control is needed, and you can see this online and when you watch television, that is if you are constantly and are always watching the news.

The Political Left just does not understand the second amendment, as they believe no person should own a gun, yet they believe they have support because of their ideology. The founders and framers of the constitution put in the second amendment due to the British government, and the role of the second amendment is for people to protect themselves from a tyrannical government, but to also provide for self-defense. Now, you will constantly hear that the Political Left does not want to take away your guns, but that is just propaganda by the Political Left.

The Political Left believes no one should have access to firearms, and they even believe many guns are weapons of war and or assault weapons because of how they look. In reality, there are no such things as weapons of war, unless you count a weapon of mass destruction. There are actually certain weapons that can be

---

[339] Ibid

converted, but these are actually prohibited to some extent.[340] Yet, the Political Left won't ever tell you that. In fact, the term assault weapon is a made up word, most likely by the Political Left, to strike fear in people.[341] A semi-automatic weapon can only shoot one round per trigger pull, while a fully-automatic weapon can actually shoot continuously.[342] However, if you are in the military, you actually use fully-automatic weapons, if you are eligible to operate such a weapon.[343] In reality, assault weapons are fully-automatic weapons, and these are usually found in the military, but there would be an extremely rigorous background check.[344] At the same time, the Political Left is also wrong, as they constantly attack semi-automatic weapons as being assault weapons, and the reason being is because of politics.[345]

You constantly hear these Political Left people, politicians, and states that there needs to be gun control, but anything that is a gun free zone actually would make that place more prone to violence because you have nothing to defend yourself. The

---

[340]Gun Facts, "Assault Weapons," Gun Facts Blog, http://www.gunfacts.info/gun-control-myths/assault-weapons/.

[341] Ibid

[342] The Blaze, "So What Is an 'Assault Rifle' Really: We Look at the Definitions and How the Term Is 'Demonized," *The Blaze*, June 13, 2016, http://www.theblaze.com/news/2016/06/13/so-what-is-an-assault-rifle-really-we-look-at-the-definitions-and-how-the-term-is-demonized-2/.

[343] Ibid

[344] Ibid

[345] Ibid

Political Left wants gun free zones, but gun free zones only benefit the criminals, as criminals never follow the laws. It is extremely and very unfortunate that the Political Left wants to take away the second amendment, but they believe it to be outdated, as they think and believe no one should have weapons, since they believe it will decrease crime. You have these gun-control groups that do not actually know the facts about gun safety and or gun rights, as their only goal is to abolish the second amendment. Gun free zones will not prevent gun violence, and passing new laws that violate the second amendment won't decrease crime. Instead, gun free zones will only help the criminals, as criminals never follow the laws, yet the Political Left does not understand this. In places where there is very strict gun control, there is high crime, and you can search this in the news websites. The Political Left does not want to admit anything, as they know they are wrong. You see, restrictive gun rights are in many European countries, and it is because they do not have a second amendment.

In fact, in any major metropolitan city in the United States, it is usually run by someone of the Political Left, and gun crime is actually high in those areas. It is because Political Left fails to even understand the bill of rights and the constitution, as they believe it is a living document. Gun crime is usually only high in those areas that are controlled by the Political Left, but that information is actually distorted by the Political Left, including the Political Left media. And then the Political Left says gun violence exists, but this is actually false. There is no such thing as gun violence, as people

182

are required to shoot the gun. The Political Left believes that the guns shoot themselves, but a gun is an inanimate object. So, in reality, guns do not shoot people. People shoot people. It should actually be called people violence, because people are killing each other. And, if the criminals have no guns but instead use some type of knife, it will probably be labeled as knife violence. But, even a knife requires a person to use it, as a knife is also an inanimate object. Everything that is a crime is committed by a person, as it is impossible for a gun or a knife to kill or stab a person by itself. It should instead be called people violence. Nevertheless, in reality, the Political Left does not care, as their true and real intentions are to abolish the constitution and the bill of rights in order to promote their own ideology.

And, to make matters worse, the Political Left wanted to undermine the constitution again when the Obama administration wanted the Senate to ratify a United Nations gun treaty for one last time before he left the Presidency.[346] Now, this UN gun treaty does actually undermine the second amendment, but the Political Left will say it doesn't.[347] And the reason why the Political Left says it does not harm the second amendment is that because they know that the UN arms treaty does indeed harm the second amendment,

---

[346] Awr Hawkins, "Here We Go Again: Obama Sends Arms Trade Treaty to Senate for Ratification," *Breitbart*, December 13, 2016, http://www.breitbart.com/big-government/2016/12/13/go-obama-sends-arms-trade-treaty-senate-ratification/.

[347] Ibid

as the Political Left hates the second amendment; and the excuse for supporting such a treaty is that the treaty actually allows gun controller to usurp the second amendment of the constitution of the bill of rights.[348] Nevertheless, it was expected that the Senate would object to ratification because of conservative Republicans controlling the Senate, and indeed the Senate refused to ratify the UN Arms Treaty because they knew it violated and could usurp the second amendment of the bill of rights of the constitution.[349] The Political Left just refuses to follow the law and the constitution, and they believe the United Nations should be superior to that of the constitution. At the same time, if the Political Left ever gains control of the Senate again, then this unconstitutional UN arms treaty could actually be ratified, and this is why the United States of America should pull out of that UN arms treaty, as it actually undermines the second amendment.[350]

In retrospect, there is also the problem of being forced to bake cakes. And if you don't bake a cake, your bakery could be shut down, and this in fact is what the Political Left does in certain states. The Political Left tried to force two Christian bakers who owned a bakery to pay a fine of $135,000 for refusing to bake a

---

[348] Ibid

[349] Awr Hawkins, "Six Obama Gun Controls President Trump Can Undo," *Breitbart*, January 26, 2017, http://www.breitbart.com/big-government/2017/01/26/six-gun-controls-president-trump-can-undo/.

[350] Ibid

cake for a lesbian wedding.[351] Now, this cake incident occurred in the state of Oregon,[352] and in the state of Oregon, they believe in communism, socialism, and Marxism, as the many of the people there are part of the Political Left. The Political Left is basically saying to pay a fine or close your business because you do not support inclusion, as the Political Left believes you cannot assert your religious views.[353] In fact, the Political Left is saying that your religious views do not matter and you have no freedom of expressing your religious beliefs,[354] basically saying you don't really have the freedom to do anything. But wait, there's more, as the Political Left basically enacted a gag order on this case, and this means that the Political Left made an attempt to block the two bakers from talking about their case.[355] Yet, the Political Left only reports on what they view are good and necessary, but let's look at the actual facts. The two Christian bakers refused to bake a cake for a lesbian wedding because it went against their religious beliefs, and this is a perfectly fine reason because the constitution through the bill of rights grants people specific rights in regards to

---

[351] Carlos Garcia, "Christians who refused to bake a cake for lesbian wedding are appealing $135,000 fine," *The Blaze*, March 3, 2017, http://www.theblaze.com/news/2017/03/03/christians-who-refused-to-bake-a-cake-for-lesbian-wedding-are-appealing-135000-fine/.

[352] Ibid

[353] Ibid

[354] Ibid

[355] Ibid

freedom.[356] Now, the Political Left has characterized these two Christian bakers as bigots and homophobes, as they refused to violate their religious beliefs; yet, when we look at the facts more closely we find that the lesbian couple was repeat customers of the bakery.[357] The two Christian bakers did not care if their customers were gay or not, as they would serve anyone, since they had no type of litmus test; but at the same time, the two Christian bakers believed doing such a thing would violate their religious beliefs.[358] In fact, if it does violate the religious beliefs of the two Christian bakers, then the bakers can refuse to provide a service, as no one can infringe on the rights of others. However, the state of Oregon did violate and infringe upon the rights of two Christian bakers, as the Political Left in Oregon made an attempt to fine the two Christian bakers because they (two Christian bakers) wouldn't comply with the Political Left's misinterpretation of the United States constitution. The Political Left constantly misinterprets the constitution and the bill of rights but that is not old news. Yet, the two Christian bakers had to close their bakery because of what the Political Left did to them.[359] Nevertheless, the madness did not end there from the entire Political Left regarding cake incidents. A person by the name of Jack Phillips is being forced to make cakes

---

[356] Ibid

[357] Ibid

[358] Ibid

[359] Ibid

for gay couples, and this is being mandated by the Political Left.[360] Now, the Political Left demands that Jack Phillips and the rest of his staff undergo some type of sensitivity training.[361] Jack Phillips and his staff were mandated to undergo sensitivity training after he lost his case in a Political Left civil rights commission and in a Political Left court in the state of Colorado; yet the Political Left demands that Jack Phillips submit quarterly updates just to see if he is in compliance with the Political Left civil rights commission, and this idiotic and frivolous reporting requirement only lasted for two years.[362] This reporting requirement was mandated by the Political Left because they do not agree with Jack Phillips's business policies, and so the Political Left believes since they don't agree with the business policies they should be changed by force.[363] The Political Left is basically saying your religious beliefs do not matter because the Political Left do not support your religious beliefs and religious freedom, but the Political Left also claims they support religious liberty.[364] Yet, the Political Left says they also support equality, but the Political Left refuses to

---

[360] Todd Starnes, "Baker forced to make gay wedding cakes, undergo sensitivity training, after losing lawsuit," *Fox News*, June 3, 2014, http://www.foxnews.com/opinion/2014/06/03/baker-forced-to-make-gay-wedding-cakes-undergo-sensitivity-training-after.html.

[361] Ibid

[362] Ibid

[363] Ibid

[364] Ibid

understand that religious liberty is a constitutional right guaranteed under the first amendment.[365] The Political Left believes that if you are asserting your right to religious liberty then you are being discriminatory to other people, as that is how the Political Left views freedom of religion, freedom of expression, and freedom of speech.[366] So, basically, the Political Left, in their case against Jack Philipps, does not view religious liberty as constitutional, but religious liberty is considered a basic guaranteed constitutional right.[367] In other words, the Political Left is saying that Jack Phillips needs to rehabilitate his behavior, his policies, and his faith, as the Political Left actually never agreed with Jack Phillips's belief, faith, and policy system.[368] At the same time, Jack Phillips has never been a bigot.[369] In fact, Jack Phillips has offered the gay couple another item for purchase, but the entire Political Left does not want to tell you that.[370] The Political Left in the state of Colorado stated it violated the rights of the gay couple, but they did not tell you it was against the law at that time for people of the same sex to get married.[371] The Political Left just wants to ignore

---

[365] Ibid

[366] Ibid

[367] Ibid

[368] Ibid

[369] Ibid

[370] Ibid

[371] Ibid

the facts, but so far they have succeeded to reduce or to repeal constitutional rights.

Nevertheless, the Political Left has also violated peoples' freedom of speech and freedom of expression, simply because that person does not believe in climate change the way that the Political Left believes in it. In other words, if you are skeptical about what the Political Left tells you about climate change, then you might be prosecuted for asserting your own beliefs, which is basically something known as persecution. Now, here is now the Political Left is going to prosecute or persecute people who are skeptical about the Political Left's view on climate change or as they call global warming: the Political Left would use racketeering laws to prosecute or persecute their climate change skeptics.[372] This is being led by none other than Political Left attorney general Eric Schneiderman of New York with help from Al Gore, yet the New York attorney general is just one of seventeen attorney generals who are doing this.[373] These Political Left attorney generals also have support and are receiving help by so-called professional climate activists, and these climate activists believe they know everything about the climate even though they don't.[374] This

---

[372] Chris Horner, "Persecuting climate skeptics: The cover-up continues," *Fox News*, June 29, 2016,
http://www.foxnews.com/opinion/2016/06/29/persecuting-climate-skeptics-cover-up-continues.html.

[373] Ibid

[374] Ibid

information indicating that the Political Left was up to no good was discovered by a FOIA request approval, but the Political Left wanted this information to stay hidden, as many of them want to obstruct public records request, and it just shows you that the Political Left is trying to abuse their power and or authority when they are in public office.[375]

Yet, it does not end there, as the Political Left climate scientists even demanded that anyone who does not believe in their view about climate change, well they should be investigated by the federal government.[376] In other words, if you have a different view of climate change then you should be investigated by the entire federal government and then possibly be charged with a criminal offense.[377] So, basically, if you have a different view in regards to climate change then you are viewed as a skeptic, yet they (the Political Left also demands you be investigated under the RICO Act for not having the same views as the Political Left.[378] That is just utter nonsense and an abuse of power, with at least one person indicating it is a politicization of science, and that is what exactly

---

[375] Ibid

[376] Judith Curry, "A new low in science: Criminalizing climate change skeptics," *Fox News*, September 28, 2015, http://www.foxnews.com/opinion/2015/09/28/new-low-in-science-criminalizing-climate-change-skeptics.html.

[377] Ibid

[378] Ibid

this is.[379] The Political Left believes there should only be one view regarding climate change: climate change is going to lead towards the end of the planet. The person behind this climate change RICO witch hunt is none other than Sheldon Whitehouse, and Sheldon Whitehouse even made an attempt to berate a solar physicist by the name of Willie Soon.[380] Now, Willie Soon has a different view in regards to climate change or what is described as global warming, as Willie Soon believes it is due to solar radiation rather than the emissions from carbon.[381]

At the same time, Political Left Sheldon Whitehouse wants to investigate the fossil fuel and oil companies, as he does not like them, since many of the Political Left believes solar and wind energy are better; and Political Left Sheldon Whitehouse wants to use the RICO Act to target supporters of the fossil fuel industries because he does not like their views.[382] Political Left Sheldon Whitehouse believes the fossil fuel industry and their supporters are misleading the public, and that is his claim to open such a RICO investigation.[383] In fact, it is the Political Left and people like Sheldon who are misleading the public, as they do not want to accept any other views. However, this abuse of power does not end

---

[379] Ibid

[380] Ibid

[381] Ibid

[382] Ibid

[383] Ibid

here, as Raul Grijalva of the Political Left in the lower chamber of Congress has also abused his position of public office.[384] Now, this person by the name of Raul Grijalva has investigated at least seven different climate scientists in Congress, yet his investigation has led to no wrongdoing by the climate scientists.[385] The Political Left partisan hack by the name of Raul Grijalva has only started this witch hunt because climate scientists are offering differing and new perspectives about climate change or what is called as global warming.[386] According to the Political Left, there is only one view on climate change—that it will lead to the destruction of the planet Earth. Even though Raul Grijalva's investigation revealed no wrongdoing, many climate scientists with a new and different perspective on climate change have been outed as pariahs because of their different views.[387]

Just by having a different perspective on climate change will lead to a political witch hunt investigation by the Political Left, but this is a problem as well as an abuse of government authority, as the Political Left wants to limit the further and future research of climate change.[388] It is important that climate change be further investigated and to offer new opinions and facts about

---

[384] Ibid

[385] Ibid

[386] Ibid

[387] Ibid

[388] Ibid

what is actually causing climate change, as we need to know all details of what actually causes the climate to change, but the Political Left rather wants to focus on an old and outdated method that is too narrow.[389]

Nevertheless, the Political Left will never learn, and they will continue to spew their false climate change hoax that it is destroying the world. No, climate change is normal, and it is part of everyday life, but the Political Left does not want you to know that, so they decide to deny everything you tell them. We must ensure that all opinions are heard in regards to climate change, as if these new and differing opinions are denied then it would lead to further the Political Left's goal of total anarchy, communism, fascism, socialism, and Marxism. At the same time, the Political Left also engages in environmental terrorism, and environmental terrorism basically targets people and places for political reasons because the Political Left environmental terrorists want to make an example of people and places. Now, environmental terrorism is actually an illegal tactic by the Political Left, as they view that the environment is under attack by people, corporations, and governments. However, that is just nonsense, as the Political Left and their political faction that supports environmental terrorism demonstrates radical extremism. And, the majority of these environmental terrorists are part of Political Left environmental terrorist organizations.

---

[389] Ibid

In December of 2014, twenty Greenpeace activists were charged with crimes for trespassing unto a UNESCO World Heritage Site, just to gain some attention.[390] Now, these twenty Greenpeace environmental terrorists were eventually jailed but then they fled justice after they posted bond; yet the UNESCO World Heritage Site these environmental terrorists trespassed on was strictly off limits to everyone, including most government officials.[391] In order to set foot on that UNESCO World Heritage Site you need special authorization but then also need to wear some type of special shoes if you are granted authorization and or approval to go to that UNESCO World Heritage Site.[392] It shows you that Greenpeace does not care about the environment, as this is just one of many reasons why they seek attention for their cause of environmental terrorism. In response to this illegal trespass on a UNESCO World Heritage Site, the government of India decided to label Greenpeace a potential threat to its economic security, as well as taking away its business licenses.[393] Greenpeace even decided to go after a company by making false claims, which is a common tactic used by the Political Left.[394]

---

[390] H. Sterling Burnett, "Greenpeace under fire," *Washington Times*, June 26, 2016, http://www.washingtontimes.com/news/2016/jun/26/greenpeace-under-fire-for-eco-terrorism-tactics/.

[391] Ibid

[392] Ibid

[393] Ibid

[394] Ibid

Now, when you dig deeper into Greenpeace, you will find out they are just promoting fear to get access to more uneducated and clueless people in order to spread their platform of environmental terrorism.[395] Most of Greenpeace consists of environmental terrorists and internet hackers, and what they do is spread flagrant dishonesty, block oil exploration, but also decided to block essential nutrients to malnourished children in many third world countries.[396] You see, we have evidence that this organization known as Greenpeace actually engages in the action of promoting environmental terrorism, but they are part of the Political Left, and so they believe it is necessary to infringe on the rights of others. Nevertheless, the Political Left also engaged in environmental terrorism, and that is when they decided to abuse the laws.

One of the latest examples of environmental terrorism from the Political Left is that of fining and or penalizing a farmer for plowing his own land; but this incident first started under the Political Left Obama administration in 2012.[397] Now, the farmer

---

[395] Henry I. Miller, "Greenpeace Is More Dishonest And Dangerous Than The Mafia," *Forbes*, June 30, 2016, https://www.forbes.com/sites/henrymiller/2016/06/30/greenpeace-more-dishonest-and-dangerous-than-the-mafia/#468ad1d84974.

[396] Ibid

[397] Tim Donnelly, "California Farmer Fined $2.8M for Plowing His Own Field," *Breitbart*, May 27, 2017, http://www.breitbart.com/california/2017/05/27/california-farmer-poster-child-for-trumps-epa-regulation-rollback-california-farmer-fined-2-8m-for-plowing-field/.

owned the land, but under the Political Left Obama administration, Obama and his members of the Political Left decided to abuse their power of public office by enacting a Political Left regulation that makes swales and wetlands property of the United States of America federal government.[398] Well now, that is certainly an abuse of power in government office, as the Political Left wants to environmentally terrorize you and take away your land if it is part of a body of water. Anyways, to get back to the point, the Political Left went after the farmer even though the farmer consulted a company to determine the appropriate places to grow and harvest Wheat.[399] Yet, the farmer was never allowed to harvest his Wheat crop because of the Political Left within the Army Corps of Engineers asserting the Clean Water Act, but in reality, the Political Left is just abusing their power; and since this is about the environment, the Political Left has engaged in what is known as environmental terrorism, because they targeted a person's actual property.[400]

In another case, the Political Left decided to do the same thing, and this time it was against an Idaho couple, and the real reason the Political Left and the Political Left decided to go after this Idaho couple was because the Political Left decided that their

---

[398] Ibid

[399] Ibid

[400] Ibid

property had protected wetlands on them.[401] Now, this was just another example of government abuse by the Political Left, and even the late justice of the Supreme Court Antonin Scalia attacked the EPA for their high-handedness regarding private property.[402] It shows you the Political Left is up to no good and they will seek to abuse their public office. The Political Left and Political Left EPA said it was illegal for the Idaho couple to fill in their land with dirt, but of course it is not against the law because the Political Left wants to make up their own laws to abuse their public office.[403] The Idaho couple owned the property and the land, and they also but eventually decided that they wanted to build a house on their parcel of vacant land.[404] Now, even though you own property and or your own land, the EPA and the Political Left do not think and or believe you should own your own land, as that is what the EPA and the Political Left basically said to the family; and so, the Idaho couple wanted to sue but the Political Left stated that the Idaho couple were not allowed to sue.[405] So now, the Political Left is basically denying due process, as the Political Left stated that the

---

[401] Becket Adams, "Supreme Court Justices 'Blast' EPA for Telling Idaho Couple They Can't Build on 'Protected Wetlands," *The Blaze*, January 9, 2012, http://www.theblaze.com/news/2012/01/09/supreme-court-justices-blast-epa-for-telling-couple-they-cant-build-on-protected-wetlands/.

[402] Ibid

[403] Ibid

[404] Ibid

[405] Ibid

Idaho couple could not challenge the decision of the Political Left EPA decision.[406] But wait, there's more, as the Political Left and the Political Left EPA believes you needed to get their approval and or permission to build on your own land, basically saying that you don't own your land because it is part of a wetlands area, and we call that legal extortion.[407] In reality, if you own your own land, you do not need permission from the federal government, as you really only need a permit from your local municipal government or whichever local governmental body is in charge of issuing housing and construction permits. Thankfully, the Supreme Court in the year 2012 unanimously in a 9-0 decision decided to overturn the Political Left decision by simply saying that people who might be subjected to wetlands compliance orders can seek judicial review of the issue.[408] The case in point of this Idaho case was that the Political Left EPA denied due process to the Idaho family, as the family wanted to challenge the decision but the Political Left said the order could not be challenged; yet, after the Supreme Court ruled, the Supreme Court basically stated that people can seek judicial review and or challenge compliance orders.[409] But, of course, the Political Left does not like defeat, and they did not like

---

[406] Ibid

[407] Ibid

[408] Ballotpedia, Sackett v. Environmental Protection Agency, https://ballotpedia.org/Sackett_v._Environmental_Protection_Agency.

[409] Ibid

that decision, because it did not fit their narrative of Big Brother, or what we know as big government. In May of 2015, the Obama administration decided to assert full ownership of all creeks, rills, streams, brooks, rivulets, ditches, burns, wetlands, and tributaries in the United States of America.[410] Basically, the Political Left thinks and believes they own all bodies of water even if it is on your own land, and the Political Left even claim that they can do this, as they claim they have the authority to assert this abuse of government power.[411] Of course, the Political Left says this new rule was necessary in order to protect the people,[412] but all it does is that it contributes to and is environmental terrorism because it tells the majority of home owners that they have no rights to their property and or land that they own.

In retrospect, thankfully the Trump administration, early on in his administration, has actually decided to review Obama and his Political Left view of enacting environmental terrorism on home owners and other property land owners.[413] But of course, the Political Left falsely claims that Trump's review order on WOTUS

---

[410] Joseph Curl, "Obama admin asserts dominion over creeks, streams, wetlands, ditches — even big puddles," *Washington Times*, May 27, 2015, http://www.washingtontimes.com/news/2015/may/27/obama-admin-asserts-dominion-over-creeks-streams-w/.

[411] Ibid

[412] Ibid

[413] Daren Bakst, "What You Need to Know About Trump's Executive Order on the Water Rule," *Daily Signal*, February 28, 2017, http://dailysignal.com/2017/02/28/qa-on-trumps-wotus-executive-order/.

will negatively impact and damage the environment.[414] Yet, the Political Left does not like Trump, as the Political Left enjoys big government, government abuse, and enacting environmental terrorism on people. In fact, this review order on WOTUS will help to end government abuse, and eventually, this Political Left regulation can be repealed and or re-written.[415] Nevertheless, the Political Left does not end there, as they believe they can enter into treaties and or agreements with foreign countries, but this power is only authorized for the federal government, and in that term, all treaties, whether binding or non-binding, well they need to be ratified by the Senate.

Several Political Left states believe they can enter into an agreement with a foreign country after Trump decided to pull out of the unconstitutional Paris Climate Accord. After news broke that Trump did confirm he would pull out of the unconstitutional Paris Climate treaty, the Political Left was outraged, saying that people will die and there will be plagues of some sort, which would then lead to the end of the world.

Now, ever since Trump's decision to pull out of the agreement, three Political Left states did state that they will attempt to enter into the Paris Climate Change Agreement at their own expense, along with eighty institutions of higher education

---

[414] Ibid

[415] Ibid

and thirty cities.[416] The Political Left billionaire Michael Bloomberg also stated that he is one of the people who is making an effort to stay committed to the Paris Climate Change Agreement.[417] And in the meantime, Governor Jerry Brown of the Political Left state of California has decided he wants to travel to the country of China to meet with climate delegates; yet Political Left governor Jerry Brown of the Political Left state of California believes California is a separate nation, indicating that he believes California is not part of the United States of America.[418] By saying that he wants California to enter into an agreement, Political Left governor Jerry Brown is asserting that he and the Political Left state of California are far more powerful and superior than the United States of America; but what is also interesting is that this Political Left governor believes he alone is the entire United States Senate and or he also believes that the state of California and its entire legislature is Congress.[419] However, the Political Left state of California is not its own separate nation and its legislature is not part of Congress, as Congress is part of the federal government and

---

[416] Tiana Lowe, "States, Cities and Firms Threaten to Unconstitutionally Enter Paris Accords Independently," *National Review*, June 2, 2017, http://www.nationalreview.com/corner/448236/states-threaten-unconstitutional-paris-climate-accords-entry-entry.

[417] Ibid

[418] Ibid

[419] Ibid

California is a state within the United States of America.[420] So, the Political Left is saying that they are above the law and above the United States constitution.

Let's make something clear, it is illegal and at the same time also unconstitutional, as states are prohibited from entering into any treaty, alliance, and or confederation.[421] The reason why states aren't allowed to enter into any type of treaty, alliance, and or confederation with any foreign country or foreign government is due to the fact that the framers wanted the United States federal government to be in charge and responsible for foreign affairs,[422] as any type of treaty, alliance, and or confederation between foreign nation is actually a binding agreement because it is part of international law.[423] Nevertheless, the Political Left believes that the Paris Climate Agreement is non-binding, as they believe it is only voluntary; but it is actually a binding agreement because of provisions within that make legal obligations binding whoever and whichever country joins.[424] In actuality, the Paris Climate Change

---

[420] Ibid

[421] Heritage Foundation, The Heritage Guide to The Constitution: State Treaties, http://www.heritage.org/constitution/#!/articles/1/essays/69/state-treaties.

[422] Ibid

[423] Ibid

[424] Tess Bridgeman, "Paris Is a Binding Agreement: Here's Why that Matters," *Just Security*, June 4, 2017, https://www.justsecurity.org/41705/paris-binding-agreement-matters/.

Agreement is unconstitutional, as it never went through the Senate ratification process, but instead was approved by the Political Left Obama administration trough the Political Left globalist supporting United Nations.

The Paris Climate Agreement is in fact a treaty, as it is a foreign agreement between at least two foreign nations as defined by the Vienna Convention on treaties.[425] In fact, the constitution of the United States of America would also call the Paris Climate Change Agreement as a treaty, as it is an agreement or compact with another foreign nation; and since that is the case it is required that the Senate ratify any agreement involving the United States and any other foreign nation, and the reasoning behind this is that the framers believed it would be considered unsafe and dangerous for just one person to have the power to enter and bind an entire country into a treaty.[426]

But, for the Political Left, well, they do not like to send any treaty involving the United States and at least one other foreign nation to the United States Senate for ratification, and this has been the case for at least two Political Left presidential administrations.[427]

---

[425] Bruce Fein, "Paris Climate Accord was no treaty," *Washington Times*, June 5, 2017, http://www.washingtontimes.com/news/2017/jun/5/paris-climate-accord-was-no-treaty/.

[426] Ibid

[427] Ibid

Something similar occurred in regards to the Paris Climate Change Agreement when Political Left president Bill Clinton decided to do the same thing with the Kyoto Agreement; and in the Kyoto Agreement Bill Clinton decided to sign the treaty in 1998 without sending it to the Senate for ratification.[428] When George Walker Bush became president, well he decided to yank the United States signature of the Kyoto Agreement just as like Trump did with the Paris Climate Agreement.[429] The reason why Bill Clinton never submitted the Kyoto Agreement to the Senate for ratification is that because he knew the Senate would have rejected that climate treaty, and so Bill Clinton decided to abuse his position of public office by signing and ratifying the Kyoto Agreement himself.[430] At the same time, President Obama did not submit the Paris Climate Agreement to the Senate for ratification because he believes in the United Nations, as Obama and Clinton were part of the Political Left who believes in a globalist agenda that undermines the constitution.

Yet, John Kerry's reasoning and or excuse of not submitting a treaty to the Senate for ratification is that treaties are hard to pass in the Senate for ratification, but from this meaning it

---

[428] Ibid

[429] Ibid

[430] Ibid

simply means that the Political Left just wants to undermine the constitution by going to the United Nations for everything.[431]

On another note, the Political Left governor Jerry Brown of the Political Left state of California decided to sign an agreement with China; yet, since the Political Left does not like Senate ratification they believe it is all legal and constitutional, but Jerry Brown is probably in violation of the constitution as well as the Logan Act.[432] This just shows you that the Political Left is up to no good, but there is more government abuse as you have seen and heard on the news.

This time the Political Left Obama administration decided to go after conservatives when conservatives filed for non-profit status for their organizations with the Internal Revenue Service. The Internal Revenue Service decided that it would get political and become Political Left, as they were notorious for abusing their power under the Obama administration. The Internal Revenue Service decided to abuse their power of governmental office by simply abusing the process. This abuse of government power and authority by the Political Left trough the Internal Revenue Service began on March of 2017 when some division within the Internal

---

[431] Patrick Goodenough, "Kerry: Iran Deal Not a Treaty Because You Can't Pass a Treaty Anymore," *CNS News*, July 29, 2015, http://www.cnsnews.com/news/article/patrick-goodenough/kerry-iran-deal-not-treaty-because-you-cant-pass-treaty-anymore.

[432] Daniel Greenfield, "The treasonous secession of climate confederacy states," *Front Page Magazine*, June 7, 2017, http://www.frontpagemag.com/fpm/266897/treasonous-secession-climate-confederacy-states-daniel-greenfield.

Revenue Service demanded applications of tea party or any type of organization similar to tea party organizations to be searched for some reason.[433] Then, in August 2010, Political Left President Obama decides to warn his supporters about some conservative and or libertarian Koch Brothers organization for running some sort of ad campaign, but then again in August of 2010 the Political Left DCCC decides to warn people and its Political Left supporters about Karl Rove type organizations.[434] Through the rest of August of 2010, the Political Left decides to attack the Koch brothers by making up frivolous claims and statements.[435] Then, when the month of September 2010 arrives, well, the Political Left decides again to attack the Koch brothers, by simply saying that the Koch brothers are using shadow groups to fund ad campaigns.[436] Now, as we continue into the month of September 2010 we find out that the Political Left keeps on attacking conservative non-profits, as the Political Left decides to say that conservative non-profits are controlled by foreign interests; but near the end of September of 2010 a Political Left Senator by the name of Max Baucus demands that the Internal Revenue Service investigate non-profits, but in

---

[433] Paul Roderick Gregory, "The Timeline of IRS Targeting Of Conservative Groups," *Forbes*, June 25, 2013, https://www.forbes.com/sites/paulrodcrickgregory/2013/06/25/the-timeline-of-irs-targeting-of-conservative-groups/#77c49fe35725.

[434] Ibid

[435] Ibid

[436] Ibid

particular Max Baucus wants the Internal Revenue Service to only investigate conservative organizations.[437] Then enter October of 2010, and we now have the Political Left actually attacking any and all conservative organizations, as the Political Left continues to spew hate and lies about conservative organizations by saying that conservative organizations are bad for America and hurts the role of democracy.[438] Let's pause for a second, as the reason is due to the fact that the Political Left actually hates conservatives, as the Political Left through Political Left president Obama has implied by saying conservative groups are bad for America, and this does imply that the Political Left does indeed hate the constitution and the bill of rights.[439] So, the Political Left and President Obama believes that conservatism is a threat to the safety of the United States of America,[440] but what this actually translate to is that the Political Left is trying to eliminate conservatism in order to replace it with Far Left Radical Extremism. Further, in June of 2011 Lois Lerner who is the person in charge of the tax exempt organization division of the Internal Revenue Service found out that conservative non-profits with such titles that contained tea party, 9/12 project, and or patriot were flagged for their name, yet Lois Lerner reportedly ordered her division to alter such practices in an

---

[437] Ibid

[438] Ibid

[439] Ibid

[440] Ibid

immediate manner.[441] Then, in August of 2011, there is some type of meeting between the chief legal counsel and the staff of the Rulings and Agreement of the Internal Revenue Service; but then near the last week of January 2012 the Internal Revenue Service decided to abuse their power again by simply targeting more organizations that seek to limit government, provides education on the bill of rights and the constitution, and to discuss the movement on social economic reform.[442] Although the Internal Revenue Service focused on organizations that seek to limit the size and the scope of government, it was also targeted against organizations who sought to expand government.[443]

Fast forward to May 2013, and Lois Lerner explains that she is sorry for what the Internal Revenue Service did but she also decided to lie again; and then President Obama decides to say that the Internal Revenue Service's targeting of conservative groups was outrageous, yet if you look back at his history about attacking conservatism, well you will find that he is probably not sorry.[444] In May of 2013 again, Political Left attorney general Eric Holder has decided to launch some type of investigation and at least one person is fired, but then Lois Lerner refuses to answer questions and then she refuses to resign so she is placed on administrative

---

[441] Ibid

[442] Ibid

[443] Ibid

[444] Ibid

leave.[445] Finally, in June of 2013 it was revealed that Political Left organizations were targeted as well and that claim was made by the Political Left Democrats, yet it was also revealed that conservative organizations were more harshly scrutinized, and this means that the Political Left Obama administration decided to attack the ideas and values of conservatism.[446] And then there is the case of John Koskinen, and this Koskinen person was stated to be some sort of turnaround artist by the Political Left Obama administration, which could be some sort of hint that Koskinen would be able to turn around the IRS targeting scandal.[447] And then emails were found in regards to Lois Lerner, yet nothing was done to punish and or reprimand Koskinen even though he knew about the emails; but for four months the Internal Revenue Service refused to answer any questions regarding the case.[448] Yet again, more emails in regards to Lois Lerner were found, but a report found evidence was allowed to be destroyed, yet the Political Left Internal Revenue Service had to explain why they covered everything up to a Congressional committee.[449] Nevertheless, no one at the Political

---

[445] Ibid

[446] Ibid

[447] Paul Jossey, "Despite Investigations, Obama's IRS Has Never Stopped Targeting Conservatives," *The Federalist*, November 1, 2016, http://thefederalist.com/2016/11/01/despite-investigations-obamas-irs-never-stopped-targeting-conservatives/.

[448] Ibid

[449] Ibid

Left Internal Revenue Service during the Political Left Obama administration was ever held accountable, as the Political Left will continue to target any conservative organizations because the Political Left hats people of different political ideology.[450] And yet, in April of 2017, a new and approved FOIA request showed that the Political Left Obama administration abused the Internal Revenue Service by targeting conservative groups, but the FOIA request also indicated that the Political Left Obama administration wanted to coerce any and all conservative groups and or organizations into giving up their rights of the first amendment so that the applications could be expedited, and this simply shows how the Political Left abuses the power of government and public office.[451]

As of this writing, there could be many other abuses of the Political Left abusing their governmental power of public office, but the Political Left media will most likely continue to cover it up and replace it non-relevant news that is false and misleading. There is a constant denial of the truth from the Political Left, as they try to always lie. The Political Left thinks that they are perfect but many times they admit that they are flawed and have committed outrageous acts. It is a perfect example of why the Political Left

---

[450] Ibid

[451] Tom Fitton, "Fitton: Documents Confirm that Obama IRS Improperly Targeted Conservatives," *Breitbart*, April 10, 2017, http://www.breitbart.com/big-government/2017/04/10/documents-confirm-that-obama-irs-improperly-targeted-conservatives/.

can never be trusted. As you have read this book, you might have arrived at the conclusion that the Political Left are just a bunch of hypocrites, but the Political Left is more than just a bunch of hypocrites. The Political Left is a bunch of bullies and liars who constantly support big government, an endless welfare state, and even an end to the bill of rights and the constitution. Now, you might say that the civil libertarians (the Political Left Democrats who oppose a surveillance/police state) are trying to prevent the government from spying on innocent Americans, but there is a problem with this narrative. The Political Left civil libertarians say they don't support a surveillance/police state because they say and always object to government spying on innocent Americans, but in actuality they are guilty of spying on innocent Americans at the same time, and this was revealed after the 2016 presidential election during the first few months of Donald Trump's historic presidency. These Political Left civil libertarians also have a hatred for the police, as they constantly berate them for doing their job, yet sometimes the police do commit crimes in which they should be held accountable for their actions, but the Political Left civil libertarians just have a hatred for the police that they are taking everything out of context.

From a political standpoint, the Political Left can be viewed as very bad and dangerous people who act in an irrational manner, but if you are just friends with them then they could be fine and dandy. Don't let anything fool you, as anyone can be actually easily deceived. The Political Left simply supports a globalist agenda and they do not care about local and regional policies and interests, even though some and or many say otherwise. Do not believe anything you hear from the Political Left, as they will attempt to use you. The Political Left has a spending problem and they view healthcare a right even though it is a privilege in the United States of America, but a single-payer system can actually ruin the financial credit of the United States of America federal government, but the Political Left just likes to spend, so they believe taxes should be raised.

On the other hand, the Political Left does not like people who have different ideologies than them. Even though the Political Left claims they support inclusion, tolerance, and acceptance, they will attempt to shut you down because you have different beliefs, values, and views than them for simply just having a different ideology than the Political Left, well the Political Left will start calling you political name slurs such as fascist, xenophobic, misogynist, Islamaphobic, racist, and sexist. Now, these words that were mentioned in the previous sentence were not supposed to be known as political name slurs, but these words became political name slurs because the Political Left started using these words for political purposes just because someone has a different ideology than them. At the same time, the Political Left hates white people, as they believe white people are the cause of all their problems, so they demand that all white people pay for reparations. But, that is not the worst part of the cultural problem, as the Political Left does not like white people celebrating foreign holidays or holidays of different cultures. The Political Left also does not like white people making ethnic foods, even though if the food item is not actually from that country. It remains something to be known why the Political Left behaves in a childish manner. The Political Left is just crazy, idiotic, and irrational.

The Political Left hates the past and they want to change and erase the history of the past, and they also demand that all white people are harming their way of life even though many of the Political Left is actually white. The Political Left does not like your right to free speech because they simply just hate opinions, views, speech, and beliefs of other people. If the Political Left does not agree with you they will call your speech hate speech, but that is just only the beginning of liberal lunacy, as the worst part is when they start to engage in actual fascism, anarchy, socialism, communism, violence, and criminal actions. The Political Left likes to protest and hold riots if they don't get their way, yet they think they are entitled to anything, including healthcare, welfare, and citizenship (if they are illegal immigrants). The Political Left just wants to abuse the role of government, and they believe any illegal immigrant should be entitled to citizenship, even though illegal immigrants did not arrive here in the United States of America in the correct manner. The Political Left will claim that healthcare is a care because it is free in other countries, but this again is irrational, as the Political Left wants healthcare to be an entitlement, and entitlements cost money. The Political Left will never give up, as they continue to demand an increase in taxes for the rich even though the rich already pays above their fair share; yet they say they believe in science but the Political Left do not want to conduct additional scientific studies regarding climate change, as the Political Left wants to continue to blame humans for destroying the climate. The Political Left does not want to conduct any new scientific studies because they are stuck in their own fantasy land. Their case regarding climate change is caused by too much carbon has been debunked by many scientists, but the Political Left will attempt to defame anyone who does not agree with their views on the matter.

Nevertheless, the Political Left has abused their power before and they will continue to abuse it in the future. The Political Left will attempt to criminalize anything, including trying to make it a crime to have a different opinion on climate change. The Political Left will attempt to take away your property by making up excuses. The Political Left will attempt to take away your freedom and your religious liberty, yet they also seek to actually undermine the constitution by simply going to the Senate. The Political Left knows they are corrupt but they continue to abuse their power and overregulate everything as much as possible, as they believe big government is good. So, for the Political Left, it is just a matter of government abuse, and they will never do the right thing for many reasons.

Conclusion

When this book was finished being written more events have probably occurred. The overall idea of this book was actually to focus on the failure of the Affordable Care Act. However, this book then transformed about the bad policies of the Political Left is bad and dangerous for America as well as the rest of the world, as the Political Left wants to make it so difficult to live in a free and open society. This book transformed into a book more about the bad and dangerous policies of the Political Left because I wanted to focus more on policy rather than just the Affordable Care Act.

As you have might learned, the Political Left does not like change, as they seek to destroy history. The Political Left does not like people of other ideologies, and if you don't agree with them, well they will try to shut you down and will call you a bigot. The Political Left is just delusional and insane. It is a perfect example of why you should avoid the Political Left, as they will seek to distort the truth.

The Political Left will make attempts to outlaw anything they don't agree with. They say they support free speech, but then you find out the Political Left only support their own free speech rights. The Political Left is never held accountable for their actions and they never seem to accept reality. When you actually find out about the Political Left you will see that they support a globalist agenda that harms the domestic and local economies of a country, as the Political Left wants to over flood the markets with foreign products. You see, the Political Left only cares about the foreign economy, as they seek to punish the domestic and local markets by supporting the policies of a foreign nation. It is indeed the Political Left does not care about domestic or local economies, as they think small business is bad.

Not only does the Political Left support a foreign economy, but they also support policies that will punish their country of residence and or nationality. Yet, it does not end there, as the Political Left likes foreign products to over flood the domestic and local markets because those foreign products are just so subsidized and cheaper in comparison than the actual product. It is a case of sadness for the Political Left.

But, the Political Left wants to give away free entitlements to anyone, but in reality the people who receive those types of free handouts; well they have not actually earned it. And to pay for this, the Political Left demands higher taxes on the rich, and they still think that the rich are not paying their fair share even though they pay most of the taxes.

Clearly, the Political Left is delusional in their decisions, as their policies are dangerous for people. Even then, the Political Left does not understand why people disagree with them. The entire Political Left just doesn't believe in the rule of law, as they seek to demand an open border society where illegal immigration should be the way of life. The Political Left just wants to support a policy that is illegal and unconstitutional, as they do not want to follow the rule of law. The Political Left seeks to criminalize anything that they don't like.

It is clear that the Political Left has lost their minds, as they are delusional. The Political Left seeks to destroy culture and they have seemed to develop a hatred for history and white people as of this writing. It is just amazing that the Political Left does not want to accept what occurred in the past. The Political Left does not want to guarantee freedom and liberty to people, yet they claim they support inclusion, tolerance, and acceptance of people of all races, creeds, nationalities, and ethnicities.

Yet, the Political Left has a different meaning of inclusion, tolerance, and acceptance, as the Political Left is only tolerant and accepting of people who agree with them. So, if you do not support the positions of the Political Left or if your beliefs and opinions are different than that of the Political Left, well they will not tolerate and or accept your views. It is something known as hypocrisy, as the Political Left only accepts and tolerates people who support their agenda.

Nevertheless, the Political Left will seek to persecute and or prosecute people for asserting their constitutional rights. It is clear that the Political Left does not support the constitution and the bill of rights, as they believe it is outdated. The Political Left is just part of a backwards society that seeks to destroy the past by ignoring it.

The Political Left just does not accept history and they see it as dangerous to their ideology. It is pretty stunning that the

Political Left refuses to accept reality and the past, but then they try to lie by saying it didn't happen that way. In reality, the entire Political Left has lost it, and they will seek to falsify information and facts just to support their agenda.

The Political Left seeks to abuse their power and authority in government, as they believe it is necessary to punish people who support the constitution. The Political Left just does not like the idea of a free society, as they rather and indeed support socialism, Marxism, communism, anarchy, and fascism. The Political Left seeks to destroy reality.

In closing, I hoped that you enjoyed reading this book, as it does offer strong evidence to support that the Political Left does not like freedom and liberty; and instead, this book reveals that the Political Left supports an abuse of government power as well as an overregulated society, but they also want to bypass the Congress and the constitution and go straight to the Political Left United Nations. I hope you had the time to read this book, as it will explain a lot of why the Political Left is not good for the world and the rest of society.

Bibliography

About Travel. Can Visitors Use Free UK Medical Services?. http://gouk.about.com/od/tripplanning/p/emergencydoctor.htm.

Adams, Becket. "Supreme Court Justices 'Blast' EPA for Telling Idaho Couple They Can't Build on 'Protected Wetlands." *The Blaze*, January 9, 2012. http://www.theblaze.com/news/2012/01/09/supreme-court-justices-blast-epa-for-telling-couple-they-cant-build-on-protected-wetlands/.

Ahlseen, Mark. "Why Government Can't Create Jobs." *FEE*, October 01, 1993. https://fee.org/articles/why-government-cant-create-jobs/.

Alexander, Rachel. "Europe Reaping What it Sowed With Open Borders Policy for Muslim Refugees." *Town Hall*, December 27, 2016. https://townhall.com/columnists/rachelalexander/2016/12/27/europe-reaping-what-it-sowed-with-open-borders-policy-for-muslim-refugees-n2263851.

American Civil Liberties Union. "ACLU takes legal action to restore DACA protections for Dreamer in Georgia." *American Civil Liberties Union*, May 23, 2017. https://www.aclu.org/news/aclu-takes-legal-action-restore-daca-protections-dreamer-georgia.

American Immigration Council. "Who and Where the DREAMers Are, Revised Estimates." *American Immigration Council*, October 16, 2012. https://www.americanimmigrationcouncil.org/research/who-and-where-dreamers-are-revised-estimates.

Associated Press. "Wisconsin students demand free college for African-Americans." *Associated Press*, February 17, 2017. http://nypost.com/2017/02/17/wisconsin-students-demand-free-college-for-african-americans/.

Australian Department of Human Services. Health care for visitors to Australia. https://www.humanservices.gov.au/customer/enablers/health-care-visitors-australia.

Australian Department of Human Services. Medicare services. https://www.humanservices.gov.au/customer/subjects/medicare-services.

Australian Department of Human Services. Pharmaceutical Benefits Scheme. https://www.humanservices.gov.au/customer/services/medicare/pharmaceutical-benefits-scheme.

Bakst, Daren. "What You Need to Know About Trump's Executive Order on the Water Rule." *Daily Signal*, February 28, 2017. http://dailysignal.com/2017/02/28/qa-on-trumps-wotus-executive-order/.

Ballotpedia. Sackett v. Environmental Protection Agency. https://ballotpedia.org/Sackett_v._Environmental_Protection_Agency.

Bandler, Aaron. "5 Things You Need to Know About 'Sanctuary Cities'." *Daily Wire*, November 16, 2016, http://www.dailywire.com/news/10816/5-things-you-need-know-about-sanctuary-cities-aaron-bandler#.

Barnert, Cyril. "No, it isn't racist to deport criminal illegal immigrants." *L.A. Times*, May 9, 2017. http://www.latimes.com/opinion/readersreact/la-ol-le-immigration-deportation-criminals-20170509-story.html.

BBC. "Migrant crisis: Migration to Europe explained in seven charts." *British Broadcasting Corporation*, March 4, 2016. http://www.bbc.com/news/world-europe-34131911.

Berrien, Hank. "Senate Democrats KILL 'Kate's Law' Ending Funding For Sanctuary Cities." *Daily Wire*, July 7, 2016, http://www.dailywire.com/news/7287/senate-democrats-kill-kates-law-ending-funding-hank-berrien.

Binder, John. "DREAMers Arrested in Nationwide Gang Crackdown." *Breitbart*, May 11, 2017. http://www.breitbart.com/texas/2017/05/11/dreamers-arrested-nationwide-gang-crackdown/.

Binder, John. "Arrest Record Puts Activist DREAMer on 'Priority' Deportation List." *Breitbart*, May 12, 2017. http://www.breitbart.com/texas/2017/05/12/arrest-record-puts-activist-dreamer-priority-deportation-list/.

Blatt, Mitchell. "Social Justice Warriors At Oberlin Don't Know Anything About Ethnic Food." *The Federalist*, January 4, 2016. http://thefederalist.com/2016/01/04/social-justice-warriors-at-oberlin-dont-know-anything-about-ethnic-food/.

The Blaze. "So What Is an 'Assault Rifle' Really: We Look at the Definitions and How the Term Is 'Demonized." *The Blaze*, June 13, 2016. http://www.theblaze.com/news/2016/06/13/so-what-is-an-assault-rifle-really-we-look-at-the-definitions-and-how-the-term-is-demonized-2/.

Bridgeman, Tess. "Paris Is a Binding Agreement: Here's Why that Matters." *Just Security*, June 4, 2017. https://www.justsecurity.org/41705/paris-binding-agreement-matters/.

Burnett, H. Sterling. "Greenpeace under fire." *Washington Times*, June 26, 2016. http://www.washingtontimes.com/news/2016/jun/26/greenpeace-under-fire-for-eco-terrorism-tactics/.

Business Dictionary. Redistribution of Wealth. http://www.businessdictionary.com/definition/redistribution-of-wealth.html.

Campanile, Carl. "Cuomo's free tuition program comes with a major catch." *New York Post*, April 11, 2017, http://nypost.com/2017/04/11/cuomos-free-tuition-program-comes-with-a-major-catch/.

Castillo, Andrea. "Here's why some immigrant activists say not even criminals should be deported." *L.A. Times*, May 9, 2017, http://www.latimes.com/local/lanow/la-me-ln-activists-deportation-20170406-story.html.

Choi, David. "Texas governor signs controversial bill targeting 'sanctuary cities' in the state." *Business Insider*, May 8, 2017. http://www.businessinsider.com/texas-sanctuary-cities-bill-2017-5.

Citizens for Tax Justice Staff. "The Five Worst Tax Policy Proposals in the 2016 Republican Party Platform." *Tax Justice Blog*, July 20, 2016. http://www.taxjusticeblog.org/archive/2016/07/the_five_worst_tax_policy_prop.php#.WStqn4zyvIU.

Crouere, Jeff. "Liberal Indoctrination Trumps Education at U.S. Colleges." *Town Hall*, December 10, 2016, https://townhall.com/columnists/jeffcrouere/2016/12/10/liberal-indoctrination-trumps-education-at-us-colleges-n2257882.

Curl, Joseph. "Obama admin asserts dominion over creeks, streams, wetlands, ditches — even big puddles." *Washington Times*, May 27, 2015. http://www.washingtontimes.com/news/2015/may/27/obama-admin-asserts-dominion-over-creeks-streams-w/.

Curry, Judith. "A new low in science: Criminalizing climate change skeptics." *Fox News*, September 28, 2015. http://www.foxnews.com/opinion/2015/09/28/new-low-in-science-criminalizing-climate-change-skeptics.html.

Delingpole, James. "Massive Cover-Up Exposed: Lying Alarmists Rebranded 70s Global Cooling Scare as a Myth." *Breitbart*, September 14, 2016. http://www.breitbart.com/london/2016/09/14/massive-cover-exposed-lying-alarmists-rebranded-70s-global-cooling-scare-myth/.

De Rugy, Veronique. "Is It Time to Repeal FATCA?." *Town Hall*, April 27, 2017. https://townhall.com/columnists/veroniquederugy/2017/04/27/is-it-time-to-repeal-fatca-n2318631.

Dishaw, Thomas. "Social justice warriors demand 'segregated spaces' at University of Michigan." *News Target*, February 24, 2017. http://www.newstarget.com/2017-02-24-social-justice-warriors-demand-segregated-spaces-at-university-of-michigan.html.

Donnelly, Tim. "California Farmer Fined $2.8M for Plowing His Own Field." *Breitbart*, May 27, 2017. http://www.breitbart.com/california/2017/05/27/california-farmer-poster-child-for-trumps-epa-regulation-rollback-california-farmer-fined-2-8m-for-plowing-field/.

Durden, Tyler. "Seattle Social Justice Warrior Demands 'Reparations' Or "We Need To Start Killing People...".". *Zero Hedge*, February 2, 2017. http://www.zerohedge.com/news/2017-02-01/seattle-social-justice-warrior-demands-reparations-or-we-need-start-killing-people.

Epstein, Alex. "97% Of Climate Scientists Agree Is 100% Wrong." *Forbes*, January 6, 2015. https://www.forbes.com/sites/alexepstein/2015/01/06/97-of-climate-scientists-agree-is-100-wrong/2/#1210523f3414.

Fein, Bruce. "Paris Climate Accord was no treaty." *Washington Times*, June 5, 2017. http://www.washingtontimes.com/news/2017/jun/5/paris-climate-accord-was-no-treaty/.

Fitton, Tom. "Fitton: Documents Confirm that Obama IRS Improperly Targeted Conservatives." *Breitbart*, April 10, 2017. http://www.breitbart.com/big-government/2017/04/10/documents-confirm-that-obama-irs-improperly-targeted-conservatives/.

Friends of Bernie Sanders. It's Time to Make College Tuition Free and Debt Free, https://berniesanders.com/issues/its-time-to-make-college-tuition-free-and-debt-free/.

Garcia, Carlos. "Christians who refused to bake a cake for lesbian wedding are appealing $135,000 fine." *The Blaze*, March 3, 2017. http://www.theblaze.com/news/2017/03/03/christians-who-refused-to-bake-a-cake-for-lesbian-wedding-are-appealing-135000-fine/.

Glum, Julia. "No free tuition for black students despite slavery reparations resolution at western Kentucky," *News Week*, April 21, 2017, http://www.newsweek.com/western-kentucky-free-tuition-black-students-587677.

Gockowski, Anthony. "White student accosted for wearing serape on Cinco de Mayo." *Campus Reform*, May 09, 2017. https://www.campusreform.org/?ID=9158.

Goodenough, Patrick. "Kerry: Iran Deal Not a Treaty Because You Can't Pass a Treaty Anymore." *CNS News*, July 29, 2015. http://www.cnsnews.com/news/article/patrick-goodenough/kerry-iran-deal-not-treaty-because-you-cant-pass-treaty-anymore.

Government of Canada. Health care in Canada. http://www.cic.gc.ca/english/newcomers/after-health.asp.

GovTrack. To pass H.R. 15073, A bill to amend the Federal Deposit Insurance Act to require insured banks to maintain certain records, to require that certain transactions in U.S. currency be reported to the Department of the Treasury. https://www.govtrack.us/congress/votes/91-1970/h255.

Greenfield, Daniel. "The treasonous secession of climate confederacy states." *Front Page Magazine*, June 7, 2017. http://www.frontpagemag.com/fpm/266897/treasonous-secession-climate-confederacy-states-daniel-greenfield.

Gregory, Paul Roderick. "The Timeline of IRS Targeting Of Conservative Groups." *Forbes*, June 25, 2013. https://www.forbes.com/sites/paulroderickgregory/2013/06/25/the-timeline-of-irs-targeting-of-conservative-groups/#77c49fe35725.

Gun Facts. "Assault Weapons," Gun Facts Blog. http://www.gunfacts.info/gun-control-myths/assault-weapons/.

Hallowell, Billy. "Muslim Group Seeks to Ban Sharia Law in America." *The Blaze*, September 13, 2011. http://www.theblaze.com/news/2011/09/13/muslim-group-seeks-to-ban-sharia-law-in-america/.

Hawkins, Awr. "Here We Go Again: Obama Sends Arms Trade Treaty to Senate for Ratification." *Breitbart*, December 13, 2016. http://www.breitbart.com/big-government/2016/12/13/go-obama-sends-arms-trade-treaty-senate-ratification/.

Hawkins, Awr. "Six Obama Gun Controls President Trump Can Undo." *Breitbart*, January 26, 2017. http://www.breitbart.com/big-government/2017/01/26/six-gun-controls-president-trump-can-undo/.

Helhoski, Anna. "Why free college isn't always free." *Market Watch*, May 22, 2017, http://www.marketwatch.com/story/why-free-college-isnt-always-free-2017-05-22.

Heritage Foundation. Guarantee Clause. http://www.heritage.org/constitution/#!/articles/4/essays/128/guarantee-clause.

Heritage Foundation. The Heritage Guide to The Constitution: State Treaties. http://www.heritage.org/constitution/#!/articles/1/essays/69/state-treaties.

Hill, Catey. "45% of Americans pay no federal income tax." *Market Watch*, April 18, 2016. http://www.marketwatch.com/story/45-of-americans-pay-no-federal-income-tax-2016-02-24.

Horner, Chris. "Persecuting climate skeptics: The cover-up continues." Fox News, June 29, 2016. http://www.foxnews.com/opinion/2016/06/29/persecuting-climate-skeptics-cover-up-continues.html.

Hunter, Derek. "Google Redefines The Word 'Fascism' To Smear Conservatives, Protect Liberal Rioters." *Daily Caller*, February 4, 2017. http://dailycaller.com/2017/02/04/google-redefines-the-word-fascism-to-smear-conservatives-protect-liberal-rioters/.

Imisides, Mark. "Chemistry Expert: Carbon Dioxide Can't Cause Global Warming." *Principia-Scientific*, February 9, 2017. http://principia-scientific.org/chemistry-expert-carbon-dioxide-cant-cause-global-warming/.

Immigration Equality. DACA (Deferred Action for Childhood Arrivals). http://www.immigrationequality.org/get-legal-help/our-legal-resources/path-to-status-in-the-u-s/daca-deferred-action-for-childhood-arrivals/.

Internal Revenue Service. "Bank Secrecy Act," September 27, 2016. https://www.irs.gov/businesses/small-businesses-self-employed/bank-secrecy-act.

Internal Revenue Service. "Foreign Account Tax Compliance Act," September 13, 2016. https://www.irs.gov/businesses/corporations/foreign-account-tax-compliance-act-fatca.

Internal Revenue Service. "Summary of FATCA Reporting for U.S. Taxpayers," November 7, 2016. https://www.irs.gov/businesses/corporations/summary-of-fatca-reporting-for-u-s-taxpayers.

ISelect. Medicare. http://www.iselect.com.au/overseas-visitors-cover/australian-health-system/medicare/.

Jones, Susan. "Pelosi: Trump 'Has No Jobs Bill'; 'They've Done Nothing'." *CNS News*, February 27, 2017. http://www.cnsnews.com/news/article/susan-jones/pelosi-trump-has-no-jobs-bill-theyve-done-nothing.

Jossey, Paul. "Despite Investigations, Obama's IRS Has Never Stopped Targeting Conservatives." *The Federalist*, November 1, 2016, http://thefederalist.com/2016/11/01/despite-investigations-obamas-irs-never-stopped-targeting-conservatives/.

Kirschbaum, Erik. "Arrest of refugee in rape and slaying in Germany threatens Merkel's immigration policy." *L.A. Times*, December

5, 2016. http://www.latimes.com/world/europe/la-fg-germany-refugee-murder-20161205-story.html.

Kottasová, Ivana. "OPEC to U.S.: Please don't pump so much oil!." *CNN Money*, May 11, 2017. http://money.cnn.com/2017/05/11/investing/opec-oil-u-s-supply/.

Licea, Melkorka, and Laura Italiano. "Students at Lena Dunham's college offended by lack of fried chicken." *New York Post*, December 18, 2015. http://nypost.com/2015/12/18/pc-students-at-lena-dunhams-college-offended-by-lack-of-fried-chicken/.

Lowe, Tiana. "States, Cities and Firms Threaten to Unconstitutionally Enter Paris Accords Independently." *National Review*, June 2, 2017. http://www.nationalreview.com/corner/448236/states-threaten-unconstitutional-paris-climate-accords-entry-entry.

Meredith, Sam. "Le Pen calls for government to immediately reinstate French borders after Paris attack." *CNBC*, April 21, 2017. http://www.cnbc.com/2017/04/21/le-pen-calls-reinstate-french-borders-attack.html.

Merriam-Webster. Definition of Fascism. https://www.merriam-webster.com/dictionary/fascism.

Miller, Henry I. "Greenpeace Is More Dishonest And Dangerous Than The Mafia." *Forbes*, June 30, 2016. https://www.forbes.com/sites/henrymiller/2016/06/30/greenpeace-more-dishonest-and-dangerous-than-the-mafia/#468ad1d84974.

Mitchell, Daniel. "Redistribution of Wealth Does Not Stimulate Economic Growth." *CNS News*, May 24, 2016. http://www.cnsnews.com/commentary/daniel-mitchell/redistribution-wealth-does-not-stimulate-economic-growth.

Mortimer, Caroline. "Laws restricting refugees' rights in Sweden spark backlash as thousands take to the streets." *Independent*, October 23, 2016.

http://www.independent.co.uk/news/world/europe/refugee-
crisis-sweden-new-law-restrict-asylum-claims-child-migrants-
afghanistan-a7376656.html.

NHS Choices. NHS in England - help with health costs.
http://www.nhs.uk/NHSEngland/Healthcosts/Pages/Prescriptio
ncosts.aspx.

NOLO. When Significant Misdemeanors Bar DACA Eligibility.
http://www.nolo.com/legal-encyclopedia/significant-
misdemeanors-affect-daca-eligibility.html.

O'Brien, Zoie. "GERMANY NO-GO ZONES: Police afraid to go into
lawless areas after open-door immigration." *Express*,
November 8, 2016.
http://www.express.co.uk/news/world/729782/Germany-no-
go-police-afraid-lawless-areas-migrants-rule.

O'Connor, Larry. "VIDEO: Head of Ambulance Union Confirms 'No-
Go Zones' in Sweden." *Weekly Standard*, February 27, 2017.
http://www.weeklystandard.com/video-head-of-ambulance-
union-confirms-no-go-zones-in-sweden/article/2007000.

Oprea, Megan G. "Don't Compare U.S. Immigration To Europe's
Migrant Crisis." *The Federalist*, September 30, 2016.
http://thefederalist.com/2016/09/30/dont-compare-us-
immigration-europes-migrant-crisis/.

Payton, Bre. "Watch A Mob Of Yale Students Bully A Professor They
Say Hurt Their Feelings." *The Federalist*, September 15, 2016.
http://thefederalist.com/2016/09/15/watch-a-mob-of-yale-
students-bully-a-professor-who-hurt-their-feelings/.

Perry, Mark J. "CBO study shows that 'the rich' don't just pay a 'fair
share' of federal taxes, they pay almost everybody's share."
AEI, June 13, 2016, https://www.aei.org/publication/cbo-
study-shows-that-the-rich-dont-just-pay-a-fair-share-of-
federal-taxes-they-pay-almost-everybodys-share"/.

Picket, Kerry. "Local Muslims Try To Shut Down Sharia Law Patrol
In Minneapolis Neighborhood." *Daily Caller*, April 14, 2017.

http://dailycaller.com/2017/04/14/local-muslims-try-to-shut-down-sharia-law-patrol-in-minneapolis-neighborhood/.

Rashid, Omar and Ashok Kumar, "More Indians eating beef, buffalo meat." *The Hindu*, October 29, 2016, updated December 02, 2016. http://www.thehindu.com/news/national/%E2%80%98More-Indians-eating-beef-buffalo-meat%E2%80%99/article16085248.ece.

Republican Overseas. GOP includes anti-FATCA and pro-RBT language in their 2016 Platform. https://republicansoverseas.com/timeline/gop-includes-anti-fatca-language-2016-platform/.

Sanchez, Tatiana. "DMV licensed 800,000 undocumented immigrants under 2-year-old law." *Mercury News*, December 28, 2016, updated December 30, 2016. http://www.mercurynews.com/2016/12/28/dmv-licensed-800000-undocumented-immigrants-under-2-year-old-law/.

Shaw, Jazz. "GOP taking one more run at passing Kate's Law." *Hot Air*, May 31, 2017. http://hotair.com/archives/2017/05/31/gop-taking-one-run-passing-kates-law/.

Shimshock, Rob. "Watch This Student Scream At A Trump Sign For Two Minutes [VIDEO]." *Daily Caller*, May 12, 2017. http://dailycaller.com/2017/05/12/watch-this-student-scream-at-a-trump-sign-for-two-minutes-video/.

Simmons, Andria. "Charge against Jessica Colotl dropped." *Atlanta Journal Constitution*, January 10, 2013. http://www.ajc.com/news/charge-against-jessica-colotl-dropped/yj5PpLBUAcWiIIol2HengK/.

Singman, Brooke. "Sanctuary Cities protests interrupt Texas House session." *Fox News*, May 29, 2017. http://www.foxnews.com/politics/2017/05/29/sanctuary-cities-protests-interrupt-texas-house-session.html.

Spencer, Roy. "Global Warming: Natural or Manmade,?" Roy Spencer PhD Global Warming Blog.

http://www.drroyspencer.com/global-warming-natural-or-manmade/.

Stafko, Chad. "Real Reasons Liberals Hate Guns." *Red State*, January 16, 2013. http://www.redstate.com/diary/stafko/2013/01/16/real-reasons-liberals-hate-guns/.

Starnes, Todd. "Baker forced to make gay wedding cakes, undergo sensitivity training, after losing lawsuit." *Fox News*, June 3, 2014. http://www.foxnews.com/opinion/2014/06/03/baker-forced-to-make-gay-wedding-cakes-undergo-sensitivity-training-after.html.

Stossel, John. "Government Doesn't Create Jobs." *Reason*, April 29, 2015. http://reason.com/archives/2015/04/29/how-are-jobs-created.

Street, Jon. "University's student government wants free tuition 'reparations' for black students." *The Blaze*, April 19, 2017, http://www.theblaze.com/news/2017/04/19/universitys-student-government-wants-free-tuition-reparations-for-black-students/.

Svajlenka, Nicole Prchal. "With S.B. 4, Texas Ignores the Lessons of Previous Anti-Immigrant Legislation." *American Progress*, May 22, 2017. https://www.americanprogress.org/issues/immigration/news/2017/05/22/432785/s-b-4-texas-ignores-lessons-previous-anti-immigrant-legislation/.

Tolbert, Alex. "Why Selling Insurance Across State Lines Won't Work." *Huffington Post*, April 19, 2016. http://www.huffingtonpost.com/alex-tolbert/why-selling-insurance-across_b_9719986.html.

Tran, Clover Linh. "CDS Appropriates Asian Dishes, Students Say." *Oberlin Review*, November 6, 2015. http://oberlinreview.org/9055/news/cds-appropriates-asian-dishes-students-say/.

United States Department of Justice: Office of the United States
   Attorneys, 1907. Title 8, U.S.C. 1324(a) Offenses,
   https://www.justice.gov/usam/criminal-resource-manual-1907-
   title-8-usc-1324a-offenses.

United States Government. Medicare 2017 costs at a glance.
   https://www.medicare.gov/your-medicare-costs/costs-at-a-
   glance/costs-at-glance.html.

U.S. Congress. Senate. *Kate's Law or Stop Illegal Reentry Act*. 114th
   Cong., 1st sess., Congressional Record 276, no 120, daily ed.
   (October 21, 2015): S.2193.

U.S. Department of the Treasury. Foreign Account Tax Compliance
   Act (FATCA), March 29, 2017.
   https://www.treasury.gov/resource-center/tax-
   policy/treaties/Pages/FATCA.aspx.

U.S. Department of Veterans Affairs. Health Benefits.
   https://www.va.gov/healthbenefits/cost/.

Wheeler, Lydia. "Republicans look to fulfill Trump's vow on 'Kate's
   Law'." *The Hill*, May 31, 2017.
   http://thehill.com/policy/335717-republicans-look-to-fulfill-
   trumps-vow-on-kates-law.

Wikipedia. European migrant crisis.
   https://en.wikipedia.org/wiki/European_migrant_crisis#cite_no
   te-13.

Wikipedia. 91st United States Congress.
   https://en.wikipedia.org/wiki/91st_United_States_Congress.

Willsher, Kim. "European far right calls for end to open borders after
   Berlin suspect shot." *The Guardian*, December 23, 2016.
   https://www.theguardian.com/world/2016/dec/23/european-
   far-right-end-to-open-borders-schengen-berlin-le-pen.

www.ingramcontent.com/pod-product-compliance
Lightning Source LLC
Chambersburg PA
CBHW071339280526
45787CB00001B/143